TWO-FACTOR THEORY: The Economics of Reality

TWO-FACTOR THEORY:

The Economics of Reality

by Louis O. Kelso
and
Patricia Hetter

VINTAGE BOOKS
A Division of Random House · New York

To MARTY AND KATIE

and THEIR GENERATION OF RISING SONS

ACKNOWLEDGMENTS

It is axiomatic that those who suffer most from ill-designed economic institutions have the least power to effect change, whereas those having the power are little inclined to correct, or even to question, a system which favors them. All the more credit is therefore due those who do not allow their own personal success to blind them to institutional defects which deny equality of economic opportunity to the majority of their fellow men.

It is impossible here to name every pioneer of two-factor economic theory in business, government, education, and the professions. The contributions of certain individuals, however, especially deserve to be acknowledged: MORTIMER J. ADLER, the first to lend the weight of his intellect and prestige to two-factor economic theory; WALTER A. LAWRENCE, who translated concepts of two-factor economic theory into the Second Income Plan, and who gave us the title for this book; DR. SALVADOR ARANETA and SEN. RAUL MANGLAPUS, of the Philippines, for their educational and political leadership in developing economies; FRANK S. CAPON, WINNETT BOYD, and JON W. KIERAN, leaders of a movement to establish universal capitalism as the national economic policy of Canada; RENÉ ÉMARD, M.P. (Vaudreuil-Soulanges, Quebec), a member of the Liberal Party of Canada, the first member of a national legislature to urge, in a major Parliamentary address, a study of the implications of two-factor economic theory for national economic policy; RICHARD S. LEGHORN, LEONARD SPACEK, SAMUEL B. STEWART (who encourages further research on means), HAROLD BANGERT, JOHN M. WINTERBOTHAM, FRANK G. CHAMBERS, WAYNE E.

ACKNOWLEDGMENTS

THOMPSON, WILLIAM E. CHATLOS, CARL H. HAAS, RICHARD E. KRAFVE, and WAYNE D. HUDSON, the vanguard of United States business leaders urging the reform of corporate strategy to accord with two-factor economic theory; PROF. GEORGE LENCZOWSKI and DR. BALDHARD G. FALK, a professional political scientist and an international economist, respectively, for their leadership urging two-factor theory in foreign development; AYLETT B. COTTON, ARCH MONSON, and LAWTON L. SHURTLEFF, for their dedicated efforts to make universal capitalism the "Republican alternative" in American politics; WILLIAM J. CASEY, the first congressional candidate to use Second Income Plan concepts in his campaign, even though their unfamiliarity may have contributed to his failure to win office; MARK GOLDES, a gifted educator, for his endeavors to introduce the concepts of two-factor theory into *academe,* where one-factor theory has heretofore reigned supreme; NORMAN G. KURLAND, who has worked tirelessly to incorporate these reforms into government antipoverty programs; WILLIAM H. RYAN, of Random House, whose wise counsel, steadfast support and able assistance were crucial to the success of this book; and finally, JAMES L. O'DELL, farmer, of Barrhead, Alberta, who cultivates his fields in summer and his neighbors' minds in winter, devoting half the year to economic toil and the other half to the work of civilization.

We are also deeply indebted to WINNETT BOYD, AYLETT B. COTTON, NORMAN KURLAND and RUSSELL JOYNER for reading the manuscript and making suggestions that much improved it. Credit for the meticulous and loving care in the typing of the manuscript through its several revisions goes to JAN HOCKETT BERTSCHE. Our task would have been vastly more laborious and complex had we entrusted this to anyone else.

L.O.K.

P.H.

July, 1967

We should be glad and not sorry when a fundamentally wrong notion of which we have been secretly conscious for a long time finally gains a footing and is proclaimed both loudly and openly. The falseness of it will soon be felt and eventually proclaimed equally loudly and openly. It is as if an abscess had burst.

—Arthur Schopenhauer

Contents

Introduction: The Illusion of Affluence

Part I:

UNIVERSAL CAPITALISM: TWO-FACTOR
ECONOMIC THEORY

Part II:

THE SECOND INCOME PLAN

INTRODUCTION:

THE ILLUSION OF AFFLUENCE

EVER SINCE THE PUBLICATION of John Kenneth Galbraith's book by that name, the "affluent society" has been a by-word for the United States. "Affluence" means, or used to mean, an abundance of material goods; an overflowing supply. Its nearest synonym is "rich." And by extension, we might suppose that an "affluent society" would be a society made up of affluent families and individuals. Such families and individuals would not only enjoy a profusion of creature comforts, but the leisure, the freedom from material care, the opportunities for self-development and creative expression, the personal security and the autonomy that characterize the lives of those who really are affluent.

But Mr. Galbraith's book, oddly enough, does not seem to be about that kind of society. Although we are assured that the people living in it are jaded with affluence, in reality they seem to display all the symptoms of *general* impoverishment. Mr. Galbraith's explanation of the facts —that the people are engaging in an orgy of consumption, kept going by an advertising industry devoted to the manufacture of unnatural and artificial wants—does not seem to coincide with the facts themselves. Affluent families and

individuals can afford to build and operate excellent schools
and hospitals—and excellent educational and medical facilities are, in fact, characteristic of affluent communities.
Affluent families and individuals can afford to dispose of
their garbage and maintain their streets—and indeed, sanitation and street maintenance are taken for granted in affluent communities. The affluent can afford good public
transportation, beautiful and spacious parks, fountains,
opera houses, symphony orchestras—and, the affluent do
in fact possess and enjoy these things in abundance. Probably an affluent people would not care to swim in a mu-
nicipal swimming pool, but would prefer instead their own
swimming pools at home or at their clubs. If the American
people in general do not have amenities of this kind, there
are only two possible explanations: either they do not
want them, or they cannot afford them and, hence, are
not really affluent.

Mr. Galbraith, like many other economists, has formed
his concept of affluence by comparing the United States
with pre-industrial economies, less industrialized economies, or nonindustrialized economies. In that sense, but
only in that sense, it may be said that the people of the
United States are affluent. However, the poverty of the past
is irrelevant to the industrial present; in terms of its productive potential, its rampant human need for an abundant
stream of goods and services, and the eagerness of its managers, engineers, technicians, and scientists to unleash the
productive power they know exists but which the economy
cannot utilize, the United States is a grossly underdeveloped
country. Under present economic misconceptions, it will
remain underdeveloped, and even retrogress.

The leading growth industry in the United States today,
aside from warfare, is welfare. During the past year alone,
the relief rolls rose by half a million people. In the past
twelve years, the number of persons receiving public as-

sistance has risen nearly 60%. (Population, during the same period, has increased about 20%.)

The 1966 annual report of the State Department of Social Welfare of New York shows that on the average, nearly one out of seventeen New Yorkers receives welfare from federal, state or local government agencies.[1] Not long ago the deputy administrator for the Department of Agriculture's consumer food-stamp program announced that when the program reaches its maximum expansion in four to five years, 4.5 million Americans will be receiving food stamps. Should we continue on our present course, the estimate will prove conservative.

Only a very sheltered observer could believe that the people receiving welfare would be able to survive without it. On the contrary, many social workers maintain that if every American qualified *by need* for welfare actually demanded it, existing governmental and charitable welfare agencies would be hopelessly inundated with claims. The argument that people are "on welfare" because of their personal vices, faults and inadequacies may flatter the self-esteem of those who advance it, but as an explanation of the causes of dependency, it will not stand careful analysis.

American personal consumer debt (including debt for housing) is now at the half-trillion-dollar level. That not only means that American families are very short of current purchasing power (otherwise they would not have to draw upon their future purchasing power months and even decades before they receive it), but that their future consumer power will be diminished by the perennial interest burden they must bear. Americans now pay about twenty-two cents out of every after-tax dollar on payment of private debt service. The bankruptcy rate continues to accelerate.

Law-enforcement officials and insurance companies

estimated for the *Wall Street Journal*[1a] that Americans would shoplift two billion dollars of merchandise during 1966. Around six hundred million dollars of the stolen goods (more than a quarter of the total) were expected to be taken from retailers' shelves during the two weeks preceding Christmas. Those statistics are a partial measure of the purchasing-power deficiency in the American economy, and the desire of affluence-starved people for the things they want and believe the economy is able to produce.

Two-fifths of a nation, or 77 million Americans, live in poverty or deprivation, we have been told, on incomes of $6,000 or less per year for families, and $3,000 or less for individuals. In a recent magazine article on consumer debt,[2] John Gunther declared that it has become "all but impossible for a family with children to live a genteel life (two cars, musical instruments) on $10,000 a year." One of the representative families interviewed by Mr. Gunther has found that an income of $23,000 per year is inadequate to maintain a standard of living that a truly affluent family would consider Spartan.

Mr. Gunther paints a vivid picture of American consumption as it really exists in homes which Mr. Galbraith and his fellow economists insist upon calling "affluent." It is consumption built upon borrowing and debt; on insecurity and fear of unemployment; on humiliation and harassment by bill collectors; on the fatigue and low morale of families where fathers moonlight and mothers work outside the home—not to fulfill themselves in careers, but because their supplementary labor incomes are essential to keep the family from sinking. Recent "multiple job-holder" studies by the Department of Labor reveal that 3.7 million known American men must moonlight at a second job in order to provide their families with that modest portion of debt-financed goods and services that constitute their celebrated affluence.[3]

The real figure is undoubtedly higher than reported because most employers and unions frown on moonlighting; it would be higher still were there not a shortage of moonlighting opportunities.

Measured in terms of gracious homes and gardens or well-appointed apartments; frequency of dining out and entertaining; personal libraries; high-fidelity music systems; original art and similar amenities; music, dancing, and language instruction; hobbies; foreign and domestic travel; good automobiles, saddle horses, club memberships; and the time and money to support generously those institutions that embody their personal interests and values (church, opera, theater, symphony, private schools, political organizations, scientific activities, civic affairs, etc.), no more than ten percent of American families, at the very outside, can qualify as affluent. Genuine affluence in the United States and in every other Western industrial economy is found only at the economy's pinnacle. Below this, like the Emperor's invisible clothes, it exists only through conventional pretense. The surfeit of consumer goods and services which Mr. Galbraith believes to exist is a mirage. The furious expenditure of money and energy in advertising, merchandising, marketing, and the like, is not, to any significant degree, the manufacture of wants, as Professor Galbraith supposes. It is a ferocious, all-out war by producers and sellers to get a bigger share of the limited and altogether inadequate consumer purchasing power in our nonaffluent society.

The causes for the disparity between the power of an industrial economy to produce wealth, and the power of the great majority of households within it to consume that wealth, lie in a series of easily correctable misconceptions about how wealth in an industrial society is produced; about the nature of the proper politico-economic goals of a free industrial society; about the appropriate financing

techniques which should be employed by business and the
banking system of such a society; and about its monetary
system. The thesis of this book is that everyone *wants* to be
affluent, that the desire is legitimate, and that general affluence *is* achievable in an economy physically endowed
with (or having access by trade to) the natural resources,
the manpower, and the know-how necessary to produce it.

As for the specific goods and services that go to make up
the affluence of any particular family, the proper criterion,
I submit, is the standard of living enjoyed by families
within the top ten percent of wealth holders or income
recipients. When this standard prevails throughout the
entire society, to the extent that it is *physically possible* to
produce this standard for every family with our available
resources, manpower, and technical know-how, we may
then, and not until then, congratulate ourselves upon having achieved general affluence. We may then say we are an
"affluent society."

My belief that the United States, Canada, Mexico, and
most of the other countries of the world are physically able
to support the sustained production of general affluence
beginning within reasonable periods of time is shared by
most business leaders, engineers, farmers, and traders that
I talk to in the course of my professional practice. In
resource-rich underdeveloped economies, it is similarly
achievable over a longer period of years, with spectacular
advances possible within three to five years.

This book is a call to the nonaffluent of all nations to
rally their forces to understand society's economic problems
and their own, and to set about, in political parties, in labor
unions, in business, and in the halls of education, to make
the very small but decisive changes that will free us to
produce what almost every human being wants: affluence
for himself and for others—a truly affluent economy, and,

ultimately, an affluent world. This book is equally a call to the men and women of all nations who are already affluent. Many of them are ideally situated, by virtue of their leadership qualifications and their positions, to bring about the institutional reforms that can create a world of affluent economies. These men and women know from their own experience that private ownership of the means of production is the bulwark of free societies and free lives. Private ownership by the many of "second economies" yet to be built is the only means of securing the private property rights they, the few, now enjoy in existing economies.

The sooner the world solves its economic problems, the sooner its inhabitants can afford leisure and peace and can get on with the nonmaterial things that are inherently important: the work of mind and spirit that is gloriously and uniquely human, the work that no machine can ever do.

LOUIS O. KELSO

San Francisco
July, 1967

PART I

Universal Capitalism: Two-Factor Economic Theory

1 UNIVERSAL CAPITALISM:

TWO-FACTOR ECONOMIC THEORY

NEVER A PRECISE TERM, "capitalism" today provides no descriptive information about any economic system, either existing or theoretical. Future generations may well wonder how ideological stances for nearly two centuries could have been fixed by a concept so functionally useless. The one true, fruitful inference that might have been drawn from the primitive industrial system that gave us the word was not drawn. The idea that inanimate things produce wealth in the same sense that animate things do, and thus can be productive surrogates for personal toil in the economic world, never dawned. Nor could it, as long as economic speculation was dominated, as it has been throughout the history of political economy, by pre-industrial mores and modes of thought that interpret all industrial reality in terms of only one of the two factors of production: man's labor. One-factor economic thought is incapable of explaining a physical world in which major productive instruments are nonhuman. This is one of the themes of our book.

Before developing that theme, however, we assure the reader that "universal capitalism" is not another feeble apology for "the concentration of capital in the hands of a few," or for "a system favoring such concentration of wealth."[4] These are dictionary definitions of the historical class capitalism that frustrates industrialization of the developing nations, and prevents Western industrial economies from consuming their own output. Universal capitalism does hold that both private ownership of the instruments of production and workably competitive markets are essential to a free, generally affluent, and leisured industrial economy. Private ownership and the free market are also tenets of historical class capitalism. But the concept of universal capitalism is not satisfied with mere private ownership of the means of production, or mere free enterprise. It also asks: *whose* private ownership? *whose* free enterprise? Not content merely to enquire into the "wealth of nations," it also enquires into the personal wealth of each of the individuals within those nations. Where productive input into the economy is made primarily by the nonhuman factor, and income outtake is based upon productive input, as it must be where the distributive principle of private property prevails, the question of the universality of capital ownership becomes paramount.

Nor does the concept of universal capitalism have any relationship whatsoever to that collection of glossy, four-color advertisements, leaflets, and statistical charts that comprise the literature of "people's capitalism." That phrase is a public-relations invention. It obscures the profound changes that private ownership has undergone and is undergoing in the United States (as in all Western industrial countries) from a people who are unquestionably committed to private ownership of the means of production, but who find it increasingly impossible to maintain that principle in an economy which distributes almost exclusively through the ownership of labor the wealth or income that capital instruments have produced.

While studies of the New York Stock Exchange show that about ten percent of American families own corporate stocks, these quantitative statistics conceal the qualitative facts. If we *functionally* define a capitalist household as one that receives at least half of the annual income it spends on consumption in the form of return on invested capital (and let us include, for good measure, capital gains from buying, selling and speculating in capital assets), *less than one percent of United States households are capitalist.*

Using phrases like "people's capitalism," "progress toward mass ownership," "modified capitalism," "progress sharing," and "modern capitalism," apologists for the status quo are fond of citing statistics which designate as capitalists the expanding portion of the population that owns homes (mostly mortgaged); private passenger cars, electrical home appliances, life-insurance policies, savings accounts, savings bonds, etc. But of the tangible items enumerated, not a single one is productive capital. Not a single one produces wealth for its owner—quite the contrary. The owner of a home, an automobile, or a television set must toil to pay for and maintain his property interest in it. He must pay insurance and taxes on his consumer possessions. As for the fiction that consumer goods can readily be converted into cash if need arises, the argument is really irrelevant, for he who does so thereby loses his useful (albeit nonincome-producing) creature comforts.

It is true that financial savings represented by bonds, insurance policies and savings accounts earn interest. But rarely does that interest more than offset the purchasing power losses these funds suffer through the inflation that, as we shall discuss later, is induced into modern free-market economies by Keynesian economic theory. Ownership of

sub-viable quantities of such financial assets does not make
a household a capitalist one. If less than one percent of U.S.
households receive at least half the income they spend on
consumption from combined capital sources, it is obvious
that no more than one percent of householders own savings in any significant amounts. Like the official stock
ownership statistics, the quantitative statistics of various
forms of savings conceal the qualitative facts.

For the past dozen years issuance of new corporate stock
has played only a negligible part in financing new plant and
equipment for U.S. corporations. The hollowness of the
claim that the United States economy is moving in the
direction of enabling "every man to be a capitalist" is
revealed by the statistics. On the average, less than five percent of new capital formation during the period 1955–65
has been financed by the issuance of securities of any kind
to the public, the remaining 95% being internally financed
(i.e., financed out of cash flow: withheld earnings, depreciation, depletion and amortization allowances, and investment credits allowed against corporate income taxes). Of
the five percent or less of total funds obtained *externally*
by U.S. corporations during that period to finance their
capital growth, less than ten percent was from the issuance
of corporate stock of any kind. Thus, less than half of one
percent of aggregate new capital formation during the
eleven years 1955–1965 came from newly issued stocks,
while 99.5% was financed through internal sources and
through issuance of debt securities that in due course must
be repaid from internal sources. In other words, 99.5% of
new capital formation of U.S. corporations during the past
eleven years was financed either from past, current, or
future *internally* generated funds, by methods which concentrate rather than broaden the ownership of those corporations that own most productive assets and produce most of
the goods and services in the U.S. economy.[5]

A growing tendency of U.S. corporations in recent years, in fact, is to use their excess cash flow to repurchase their own outstanding stocks. This, combined with the effect of sales of individual stockholdings directly or indirectly to institutions, resulted in an average decrease in corporate stock held by individuals of 2.3 billion dollars in each of the years 1959–63, in spite of the mere numerical increase in U.S. stockholders during those years from *12.5 million* to *17 million*.[6]

In the phrase "universal capitalism," the word "universal" means approximately what it does in the phrase "universal suffrage." It refers to an economic system in which all citizens (either as members of families or as individuals) own or have effective opportunity to own viable holdings of productive capital, and in which the opportunity to acquire legitimately such holdings as legally protected private property is acknowledged as an indispensable social goal, personal right, and essential pre-condition to any genuine equality of economic opportunity. It is true that such an economic system has never existed.[7] Prior to the publication by Kelso and Adler of *The Capitalist Manifesto* in 1958, neither the goal of universal capitalism, nor an effective means for achieving it, nor the compelling reasons for *all* men to demand it, had been formulated. In that book the authors recognized that the nonhuman factor of production—capital (productive land, structures and machines)—produces wealth in precisely the same sense as human labor, and therefore that the ownership of capital instruments is potentially an income-producing supplement to, and even substitute for, personal toil in the real economic world.[8]

Though in essence this idea is simple, its implications are far-reaching. The acceptance of capital as a co-factor of production gives to economic thought an unsuspected third dimension, and opens a new window on history. We begin

to understand that historically the word capitalism has
never described a "system" but, rather, has been a behav-
ioral term describing the accidental concurrence of certain
widely varying phenomena; we begin to suspect that under-
neath the shifting panorama there may exist a rational concept that would enable us to enjoy the proven benefits of
historical capitalism without the intolerable defects, equally
well proven, that constitute the negative case of the Marxian
socialists. That concept, the theory of universal capitalism,
is the subject of *The Capitalist Manifesto* and its com-
panion volume, *The New Capitalists*.[9]

The theory of universal capitalism introduces symmetry
and logic into an industrial economy where the bulk of
wealth is produced, not by human labor as under pre-
industrial conditions, but by capital instruments. Its economic objective is the production and enjoyment of the
highest level of affluence (humanly useful goods and services) for every family, consistent with optimum use of the
economy's resources and productive power, and the desire
of its people to consume. The political objective of universal
capitalism is maximum individual autonomy, the separation of political power wielded by the holders of public
office from economic power held by citizens, and the broad
diffusion of privately owned economic power.

2 UNIVERSAL CAPITALISM:

SOME ASSUMPTIONS

IN ADDITION to its main premise that capital and not labor is the source of affluence in an industrial society—indeed the only possible source of affluence in any free industrial society—the theory of universal capitalism is based upon certain other assumptions.

Economic Assumptions

(1) Mass production implies mass consumption; it is illogical to build the industrial power to produce goods and services without building at the same time the commensurate economic power of families and individuals to consume the output.

(2) Where millions of families are downright poor and the vast majority of the rest live well below the standard that is physically feasible, the realization of general affluence, even in such advanced industrial economies as the United States and Canada, will require an economic growth rate of several times the three and a half or four percent that is currently achieved in the U.S. and in most Western economies. That growth must represent real increases in

the economy's power to produce consumer-useful goods and services, not make-work ones such as excessive munitions, space hardware, supersonic transports (when over 90% of the population is too poor to use our present subsonic jet airplanes), etc. Measures that do not increase the output of consumer-useful goods and services, but which create additional purchasing power or redistribute the purchasing power arising from production in the existing economy, have no possibility of bringing about the vast new capital formation, the "second economy", necessary to produce genuine affluence for everyone.

(3) Production and consumption in a market economy form a natural equation. That is implicit in Say's Law, which holds that in a market economy the aggregate market value of the wealth produced is equal to the aggregate purchasing power created by the process of production.[10] The problem is one of structuring production in such a way that every household has an opportunity to make a viable productive input into the economy, thereby automatically entitling it to receive purchasing power equivalent to its productive contribution.

An Ethical Assumption

The theory of universal capitalism is based on assumptions about human nature: All men want to *produce* the wealth they and their families wish to consume and enjoy; no one wants his livelihood to depend on the arbitrary will of others; everyone hates to receive charity; everyone despises a parasite. These human sentiments seem to be universal. In the injunctive form they make up the Puritan ethic, the Marxian socialist ethic, the Confucian ethic[11]—indeed, the social ethic of all people who have aspired to live together in peace and mutual respect.

Assumptions About the Good Society

The theory of universal capitalism makes two assumptions about the good society. One is that its most important value is freedom. Any society seriously caring about freedom must structure its economic institutions so as to widely diffuse economic power while keeping it in the hands of individual citizens. Nor can freedom in an industrial democracy be long maintained unless the economic well-being of the majority is reasonably secure. Never in history has universal suffrage been built on a sound economic foundation; it is this defect, not the ordinary man's inability to cope with freedom, that accounts for the notorious fragility of democratic institutions.

Secondly, it is assumed that leisure is essential to a civilized definition of affluence. To venerate collectively what every intelligent man eschews individually, namely unnecessary toil for the goods of subsistence, makes no human sense. Today, in Western industrial society, we see toil advancing totalitarian claims on the whole of life at the very moment in history when technology offers liberation. Leisure and the liberal-arts tradition are giving way to the totalitarian work state which has no place for whole men, only "human resources" and servile functionaries. The totalitarian toil state originates in the propertylessness of the majority, as the German philosopher Josef Pieper understands.[12] Like freedom, leisure cannot survive in an industrial society if distributive institutions doom the majority to toil, either real or pretended.

3 THE TWO PRINCIPLES

OF DISTRIBUTION

THE HEART of an economic system is its principle of distribution. Real wealth is goods and services; its production takes place in the physical world under natural laws that are everywhere the same. Regardless of an economy's political structure, production problems must be solved pragmatically through science, engineering, technology, management and the skills of labor. Out of the production process, however, arises wealth or income, and distribution of this wealth or income involves problems of a different order. There is a political dimension to distribution as well as a physical one; its character is derived from the economy's principle of distribution.

Upon the choice of distributive principle turns, for good or ill, an economy's ethical, motivational, and even engineering characteristics. In the long run, the distributive principle will control the quality of life obtainable in the society—not only material abundance, or lack of abundance, but also such intangibles as the presence or absence and degree of personal freedom, justice, leisure, autonomy, and social cohesiveness.

Contrary to the popular belief that there are many

distributive principles from which economic policy-makers may select, in the absolute sense there are but two. They are diametric opposites, both logically and in their social effects, so that an economy cannot escape its moment of truth by choosing both. Attempts to mix or blend the alternatives, like any attempt to mix diametric opposites, can only produce varying degrees of confusion and foment strife between wealth or income claimants who would benefit more under one principle than the other.

The first alternative is the principle of private property. The second is the principle of need. To fully appreciate the difference between them, we must first understand the two senses in which we commonly use the word "need." As a condition of life, "need" refers to the animal nature of man and his creature-comfort requirements. If man did not have needs in this sense, that field of intellectual endeavor known as economics would not exist. As a principle of distribution, however, "need" has an entirely different meaning. It refers to the mechanism for allocating wealth or income among various claimants not on the basis of the productive input of those who participate in production, but on the basis of an opinion or appraisal of the "need" of the recipient, whether or not the recipient participated in the productive activity, and irrespective of the extent of that participation, if any.

The theory of universal capitalism relates, as does all economic theory, to the satisfaction of need in the first sense. *But it is intended, over a period of time, virtually to eliminate the necessity for distributions according to need in the second sense.*

Up to now, Western society in its public philosophy has overwhelmingly preferred the private property principle— that wealth belongs to those who produce it. The reasons are solidly pragmatic. *Before an economy can have a distribution problem, there must be a product to be distri-*

buted. No other incentive is so well calculated to keep people permanently interested in doing those things that
encourage production as that which gives to each man the
wealth, or its income equivalent, that his labor or his
property has brought into being.[18] The indispensability of
private property to the diffusion of (economic) power is
axiomatic in Western political thought, as is the necessary
relationship between private property and civil liberties.

"To each according to his production" strikes a deep
moral chord in human nature. Almost everyone instinc-
tively feels, at least in his own case, that this rule is right.
Everyone, when deprived of the fruits of *his* production,
feels heinously ill-used. The private property rule is em-
braced by the Marxian socialist no less firmly than by the
Puritan capitalist (although, as we will point out later, the
socialists insist upon the dogma that there is but one factor
of production: labor). Private property is also the ethical
heart of the labor movement, and the basis for the proposition that every man not a slave owns his own labor power
and is thus entitled to receive, *as of right,* all of the wealth
his labor produces. Related to this principle is the feeling,
also universal, that every man has the obligation to produce
the wealth his household desires to consume.

The private property principle has a unique practical
value. It makes possible the employment of the only possible objective standard for determining economic value
and, therefore, distributive shares: the workably competitive market. Without an objective standard of measurement, a scale in which to weigh the value of input and outtake, distributive decisions ultimately must be settled by
brute force or made by an authoritarian human judge.

The second alternative principle of distribution disre-
gards productive input; its determinant is human need. Although earlier the philosophy of the Diggers of Cromwell's
Army and of the French Utopian Communists, the practical

importance of the need principle began with the Marxists. In the higher phase of Communist society, Marx wrote, after society had been cleansed of the taint of selfishness it had acquired in the capitalist womb, the narrow bourgeois horizon of rights (i.e., the private property principle) would be left behind, and society could enscribe on its banner: "From each according to his capacity, to each according to his need." Socialism was a necessarily totalitarian interim stage designed to purge man of his acquisitive instinct. For Marx and the early Marxian scholars clearly understood that an economy could not function under such a form of distribution as long as man retained any trace of selfishness. Modern exponents of the need principle have abandoned that shrewd insight. They advocate the current distribution of more income to all (save the presently affluent) solely on the grounds of the general *need* for more income.

"To each according to his need" is of necessity a totalitarian principle. Its coercive nature is demonstrated by the fact that wherever it is found in society—in the extended family, the primitive tribe, the military unit, or the religious order—the organization of the distributive group is authoritarian and its members constrained to obey. Where democratic ideals preclude authoritarianism, for example, in utopian experiments like Owenism, petty bickering over "sharing" (i.e., distribution) eventually breaks up the group. Applied to a national economy, the need principle compels administration by government; only the state is sufficiently powerful to enforce a rule so at odds with human nature and to quell the resultant social strife. For the need principle, as Marx foresaw, is unworkable so long as men remain even slightly selfish. Moreover, society has only two chief sources of manipulatory power other than the brute force of the military. These are *political* power and *economic* power. The need principle fuses the two into a monolith because those who determine economic need are the same public

office holders who wield the society's political power. In the
practical sense, their power is totalitarian because no other
domestic force is strong enough to match it or temper it.

A theoretical alternative to a central arbiter is to allow
every man to decide his own need. But that course swiftly
leads to social disorganization, for each decides his needs
disproportionately to what is available in the aggregate, or
to what others decide for themselves. And since such chaos
is intolerable to society, the state is obliged to step in with
the totalitarian corrective.

There is another reason why the need principle arouses
antagonisms so violent that they must be checked by force.
It destroys the property rights in wealth that are naturally
asserted by those who own it. The owners can never be
reconciled to parting with their property on account of the
need of another, unless they receive equivalent compensation. Niccolò Machiavelli warned his Prince that "men for-
get more easily the death of their father than the loss of
their patrimony."[14] Alexis de Tocqueville understood that
the passions created by property are most keen in democ-
racies, particularly among men of the middle classes.
Those who would remedy society's injustices by means
that invade property, however obliquely, would do well to
meditate on what De Tocqueville says on the subject:
"But the men who have a competency, alike removed from
opulence and from penury, attach an enormous value to
their possessions. As they are still almost within the reach
of poverty, they see its privations near at hand and dread
them; between poverty and themselves there is nothing
but a scanty fortune, upon which they immediately fix
their apprehensions and their hopes. Every day increases
the interest they take in it, by the constant cares which it
occasions; and they are the more attached to it by their
continual exertions to increase the amount. The notion of
surrendering the smallest part of it is insupportable to

them, and they consider its total loss as the worst of misfortunes."[14a] Not only are people attached to their property because it is the only dependable source of comfort, security and status in a world where, as George Orwell said, ". . . the belly comes before the soul, not in the scale of values but in point of time!"[15]—but because the economically productive resent supporting the unproductive, even when incapacity is due to no personal fault—or is even the direct result of service to society, as in war.

Unlike the private property principle, the need principle has no intrinsic limitations, either physical or logical. Private property is objective and specific; need, subjective and universal. Under the rule of private property, a claimant is entitled only to the equivalent of his production; this is a built-in check that automatically proportions demand to what is available. Private property enforces productive responsibility; it establishes orderly, dependable relationships between men, and between men and their environment. The need principle, by contrast, abolishes personal productive responsibility, severs dependable property relationships, and provides no mechanism to relate the size of the product to the demands of claimants. Thus the underproductive or nonproductive may claim any part of the product or even all of it, in the name of their human need (i.e., their unpurged selfishness). Needism acknowledges no geographical boundaries. Under its logic, as the United States is becoming more and more urgently reminded by its needy neighbors, the poor nations have a moral claim to the wealth of the rich nations, no less than the poor within each rich nation have a moral claim to the wealth of their own productive countrymen. The international effects of the need principle are the same as the domestic effects: hatred, strife, violence, and the decay of productive motivation.

4 THE NEEDISTS[16]

"NEEDISM" is our proposed term for a body of economic thought flourishing today under a variety of names across the entire political spectrum, which has yet to be formally identified as a school, unified by one central idea. The idea is not new; only its popularity is. The upsurge began when J. K. Galbraith, recognizing that economic output in the U.S. economy had become subordinate to income and employment, launched his search for a "device for breaking the nexus between production and income security."[17]

At face value the proposals for eliminating poverty that emanate from this school seem heterogeneous. They include the guaranteed income of the Ad Hoc Committee on the Triple Revolution;[18] "The American Dream" of Richard Cornuelle, calling upon corporations and associations to take over more of the growing welfare burden of government;[19] the negative income tax;[20] expanded social security; income subsidies disguised as prolonged education; government employment of the otherwise-unemployed; accelerated and broadened welfare programs; the guaranteed life income visualized by some labor unions;[21] universal maximum unemployment compensation;[22] the surplus food-stamp program; government subsidies to agriculture, mining, and industry, and such earlier proposals as Social Credit's national dividend (see footnote 27a). But diverse as they may seem, all these concepts are based upon the distributive philosophy of the old utopian maxim: "To each according to his need."

The number of ways in which purchasing power may be diverted from those who produce the economy's useful goods and services, either through their labor or through the productive input of their privately owned capital, is virtually unlimited. That is to say that while there is but a single logical way in which outtake can be related to input, there is no logical limitation upon the variety of ways in which input and outtake can be *unrelated*. The following categories by no means exhaust the ingenuity of needist thought.

(1) Some Needists emphasize the infinite potential of government employment. As Professor Parkinson so delightfully documents, the world is growing more and more inured to governmental employment that neither accomplishes any useful human purpose, nor is intended to.[23] We estimate that of the eleven and one half million employees (exclusive of the military) on government payrolls in the U.S. today, in excess of three million are engaged in various forms of redistributing wealth and income.[24] The ambitious politician naturally favors increased government employment because of its enormous possibilities for patronage, for "buying votes," and for perpetuating a political administration through the economic dependence of constituents. Since government make-work employment is supported by taxation on the sector of the economy that produces useful goods and services, it may be classified purely and simply as redistribution according to need.

(2) Some needist proposals take the form of growth worship. Of course, anything that increases the gross national product may provide some increases in employment. How-

ever, growthmen are careful not to inquire whether the employment their proposals will create is legitimate employment—that is, employment necessary to the production of useful goods and services, or even employment incidental to the proper and necessary functions of government, as distinguished from government employment required to effect needist redistribution. For example, they do not ask whether producing farm surpluses is not, in intent and effect, a policy for giving farmers more income because they *need* more income. (The surpluses themselves can also be given away to the poor because they *need* food.) Nor do growthmen appreciate having their proposals questioned on the grounds that increases in the GNP often represent goods and services not only useless to the human race, but inimical to it. Examples would include many kinds of stockpiles accumulated by government and periodically destroyed; the production of space-race hardware that cannot possibly justify its priority as long as the world's main problem of providing useful goods and services necessary to eliminate poverty remains unsolved, etc. Growthmanship Needists also are proponents of monument-type public works; of public projects that would be overwhelmingly rejected by the taxpayers to be saddled with the payment burden if submitted (according to accepted democratic principles) to popular vote.

The dedicated growthman is not much concerned about the quality of what is produced as long as its production creates employment. He is not concerned with the resources so lavishly wasted in the process of maintaining artificial toil. Nor is he concerned with the effect such policies have on the incentive to produce. He is not concerned about the use of the thing produced, or whether it has any use. Bread or napalm—it is all the same to the Gross National Product. The construction of defense systems known to be obsolete before they are begun, the subsidizing of pointless research, and the generation of mere inflation—these are some of the model tools of growthmanship.

Nothing emanating from the growth-for-growth's sake group is designed to raise the economic *productiveness* of the income-needy who are the nominal beneficiaries of its proposals. If the assumptions of universal capitalism are correct, there is only one way to increase the productive power of most individuals: by enabling them legitimately to acquire the ownership of productive capital in the process of bringing new capital formation into existence. No such proposals are made by the needist proponents of growthmanship.

(3) Some Needists openly advocate featherbedding, i.e., pretending to work without producing anything. Recognizing the psychological need to be productive, and the human hatred of being a ward of charity, they encourage the appearance of useful employment gutted of its reality.

(4) Some Needists concentrate only on the mechanics of redistributing income from those who produce it to those who, in the redistributors' view, need it. Again the means are various. One faction may emphasize ease of administration; thus it will favor the method that is most administratively efficient, even though the hated charity or welfare principle is openly exposed. The negative income tax (an avant-garde euphemism for a positive income dole) is a case in point. It is claimed that direct payments to those whose incomes fall beneath a certain floor would eliminate the vast costs of administering welfare schemes more graciously disguised. These "costs," however, represent the wages and salaries of the welfare administrators. Eliminating the one would eliminate the other. Shorn of their professional employment, most members of the welfare bureaucracy would thereupon quickly qualify to receive the

very "services" they formly dispensed. Another Needist faction may advocate that method which most cleverly conceals the alms basis of redistribution, even at the price of a complex and cumbersome administrative procedure and the opportunities for fraud and graft that such complexity generally entails.

(5) Other Needists play on the Horatio Alger awe of education. They attempt to disguise vast *need distributions* as subsidies to education, or government-sponsored research or tax-supported retraining, either for jobs that must be synthesized through subsidy or for real jobs that, in the judgment of the business world, are best learned by on-the-job experience. The heavy shift from liberal arts education to vocational training, with special emphasis on those branches relating to synthesized tax-supported vocations (space scientists, professional researchers, welfare workers, etc.), demonstrates the spectacular progress made in recent years by the educational Needists.

(6) Still other Needists specialize in redistributive non-work compensation. This concept involves paying repeatedly for work performed once, if at all. Techniques invented so far include permanent and universal unemployment "compensation," "earned leave," economic security by "right," automation pensions, guaranteed annual retirement payments, etc.

(7) Some Needist solutions benefit the affluent far more than they help the poor. Take, for example, the government stockpiling of humanly useful goods such as agricultural surpluses, pharmaceuticals, machine tools, and other goods that are produced with high capital input and relatively low labor input. "Creating" employment by governmental subsidy of capital-intensive industries is, as we will emphasize later, far more beneficial to the owners of concentrated holdings of capital than to the employees, other-

wise incomeless, who are thus given wages because they *need* them.

(8) Still other Needists would disguise the use of the need principle by automatically raising wages from time to time through legislation and other coercive measures. Such wage increases are justified, it is explained, by the "rising productivity of labor." But the facts reveal that there is no corresponding increase in labor input; in virtually all cases, actual labor input decreases. The "productivity of labor" is rising because it is defined as "increase in output per man-hour." But the cause of the increase is *invariably* additional and/or more efficient capital instruments.

The rhetorical use of the private-property principle of distribution to disguise needist redistribution by attributing it to the rising productivity of labor is nowhere better illustrated than in the "wage guidepost" officially advocated by the U.S. Council of Economic Advisers since its Annual Report of January, 1962. "The general guidepost for wages is that the *annual rate of increase of total employee compensation (wages and fringe benefits) per man-hour worked should equal the national trend rate of increase in output per man-hour.*"[25]

Interpreted in the light of the fact that the physical cause of all increases in output per man-hour is improved capital instruments and additional capital instruments being put into production, thus increasing output per man-hour more than enough to offset declines in the actual labor input per man-hour, the wage guidepost is nothing but an official sanction of the needist doctrine of distributing the increased output produced by capital to the nonowners of capital, i.e., labor, on the basis of labor's recognized need for more income. Stated another way, *the wage guidepost is a formula for the relentless erosion of private property*

*in capital, since the essence of private property is that it
entitles the owner to receive the wealth produced by what
is owned.*

Now that labor unions, driven by the inadequacy of
one-factor solutions, are repudiating the wage guidepost in
the United States and corresponding wage guidelines in
other economies in favor of even more radical measures of
needist redistribution, it is clear that either (1) the rate of
erosion of private property in capital will accelerate, moving those economies more quickly toward total economic
communism or, (2) the erosion of private property in capital will be slowed down through increasing profit margins
on goods and services, thus bringing about spiraling inflationary prices.

At this point, one thing must be made clear. We fully
agree that labor *does* need more income. Since affluence is
the product of the nonhuman factor, only a few highly paid
professionals would be able to produce, under competitive
conditions, an affluent level of living through their labor
power alone. The only rational overall goal for an economy
is that of universal capitalism: general affluence. Until that
goal is achieved, any individual or any family that is not
affluent (if the economy is physically able to produce affluence for all) *does* need more income.

5 NEEDIST SOLUTIONS:

SOME PROBLEMS

IF NEEDIST REDISTRIBUTION TAKES the form of coerced
or legislated wage increases in the useful-goods industries,
it bloats consumer prices with welfare costs; thus, to the
extent the increased distribution to labor (not being accompanied by any increase in productive input *by labor*) is
not absorbed by the capital owners at the cost of the erosion
of their property rights, the benefit takes the form of inflation and is illusory. Paying a worker more for the same or
less labor input does not increase the available consumer
goods and services which *he* produces.

If redistribution takes the form of coerced or legislated
wage increases in the useless or noneconomic goods industries (such as the space race, military overkill hardware,
etc.), the effect is purely inflationary to the extent that the
wage increases are not offset by corresponding income tax
increases. The purchasing power which arises out of the
production of useless goods and services is not matched by
an equivalent supply of consumer-useful goods and services,
which are the only kind that satisfy creature comforts.
Therefore, in the pockets of individuals, it will be spent to
bid up the price of useful goods and services. The net effect

is to broaden the distribution of poverty, rather than to increase the number of families who enjoy affluence.

If redistribution takes the form of direct money doles to individual consumers, such as welfare checks, guaranteed annual income payments, or negative income tax distributions, with taxation on middle and high incomes or increases in government debt supplying the funds, some income otherwise invested will be diverted to consumer goods and services. But the apparent increases in the gross national product will be mostly inflationary (i.e., imaginary). An indispensable condition for building a genuinely affluent economy is new productive power. Redistribution is incapable of bringing into existence any significant amount of new capital formation.

If redistribution according to need takes the form of direct governmental distributions of goods the government has bought previously (such as goods surpluses), the path is paved for habitual government purchase of such goods; thus, as noted above, the concentration of ownership of productive capital is further promoted. The resulting economic patterns are familiar throughout the nonsocialist Western world. It is true that the most dire forms of poverty may be somewhat diminished through this process, but the poor are still never enabled to become affluent. No man has ever achieved affluence on a dole, nor will he.

Needist schemes have another inherent shortcoming that none can avoid. Its most familiar manifestation is the "means test," presently found in all welfare laws and arrangements. The recipient is required to demonstrate, as a condition to his dole, the nature and extent of his need. Thus the human dignity of the recipient, already wounded by having to apply for charity, is dealt a second blow. On humanitarian grounds most modern needist schools propose that the means test be abolished, and that all humans be granted a legal or constitutional right to some kind of income without productive responsibility. Expedients of various kinds may succeed in disguising the means test temporarily, but they will never dispose of it—the problem goes deeper than the Needists suppose.

Experience shows that, as a general rule, human beings are incapable of judging the needs of others to be as great as their own. To put it another way, every human being desires affluence for himself but few, if any, having the power to bestow or withhold, believe that this need is equally valid for others, particularly when those "others" are strangers. Exceptions to this harsh rule are rare, as any estate lawyer can testify. During their lifetimes and in their last wills and testaments, the wealthy almost unfailingly appraise the "needs" of their children, grandchildren, relatives, friends, and employees as being well below the levels of consumption they considered desirable, and even necessary, for themselves during their own lifetimes; frequently they prefer to give the bulk of their fortunes to charities and foundations in which they have evidenced little previous interest. Many potential heirs live on their expectations for decades, rear their families in genteel penury, and are well past middle age when their inheritance finally devolves upon them.

A Joseph Kennedy who gives each one of his children a million dollars upon their majority because he wants them to be independent even of him astonishes the world precisely because the sentiment is so uncommon. Even old family retainers who have given a lifetime of faithful and unselfish service are seldom left with more than a symbolic pittance by the departed objects of their devotion. As for those who give generously of their wealth to strangers, they are in every age the stuff of legend and sainthood.

The historical lesson is clear: the needs of persons not

objects of natural bounty will always be appraised as minimal. The productive will never voluntarily support the unproductive in an affluent style. They never have, and the evidence is that they are emotionally incapable of it. Even the Soviet Union has its antiparasite laws, and its constitutional mandate that those who do not render society productive labor shall not eat. Thus distribution of wealth according to the need principle—so offensive to society in practice—is indefinitely postponed to those distant aeons, calculable only in astronomical magnitudes of time, when the acquisitive instinct, according to the Marxist intellectuals, shall have been purged from human nature.

The most important generalization that can be made about *all* needist proposals is that they invariably address themselves to the *effects* of poverty, i.e., insufficient income, rather than to the *cause* of poverty, i.e., low productive power of the poor. Needist solutions in general are either proposals for further steepening pinnacle affluence, or for equalizing poverty. They are not, and by their very nature cannot be, instruments for achieving the ideal goal of universal capitalism, which is universal affluence. That goal can be achieved only by universal capitalism and practical steps for its realization of the tenor of those contained in the Second Income Plan. They alone are designed to enlarge the physical economy, to bring into existence a capital plant (in the United States and in Canada, for example) several times as productive as those presently in existence, and to structure the financing of these second economies so that they will be owned by the 90% of families and individuals who do not own viable capital holdings in either of these economies today.

The less the incentive to produce, the smaller the product. To the extent that Needists succeed in redistributing income and wealth from those who produce to those who do not, they kill the incentive to produce. Laws will not substitute for that incentive. That is why the British laborer works about 20% of his time on the job. That is why the Soviet Union, fifty years after its great social revolution, cannot adequately feed, house or clothe its people. That is why many citizens of redistributive Sweden must wait ten years or longer for an apartment or house, etc.

The nations of the world may take years and even decades to recognize as needist proposals many schemes that are verbally, legally, politically, or psychologically disguised. But in a world in which all men want affluence and most, if not all, could produce it through the combined forces of labor and capital, needism as a principle of distribution is doomed. Needism is contrary to human nature: it cannot work, and it will not work. It can only foment bitterness, enmity, strife and disillusionment in the societies that undertake the experiment.

6 UNIVERSAL CAPITALISM AND CONVENTIONAL ECONOMICS

ALTHOUGH THEY ADVOCATE different means for reaching it, and differ about many other particulars that weigh heavily in government, business, and academic debate in the United States and in the Western economies generally, the three principal schools of conventional economics espouse the same economic goal: *full employment.*

If the government will keep its hands off interest rates, wage policies and the economy in general (laissez-faire), assert the classical (i.e., nonsocialist) economists, the "unseen hand" of the free market automatically will achieve the wisest resource use and guide the economy to equilibrium at full employment and prosperity.

All wrong, contend the socialist (Marxist) economists. Full employment and its resultant prosperity for all workers (and everyone must be a worker) are achievable only by eliminating private property in capital and substituting state ownership "for the benefit of the whole society."

The Keynesians disagree with both the classicists and the Marxists. They insist that full employment can best be achieved by increasing (to whatever extent necessary because the end justifies the means) "aggregate consumer demand" through deficit financing of government expenditures, by raising wages above their free-market level, and by virtually any other government-sanctioned redistributive technique that adds purchasing power to the workers and to the unemployed.[26]

The theory of universal capitalism challenges the classicists, the Marxians and the Keynesians precisely on the point on which they all agree: *the goal of full employment.* Universal capitalism rejects this goal as (1) humanly repugnant; (2) functionally inadequate and, (3) socially perilous. Employment in producing economic goods and services is not an end in itself. It is only a means to an end. The human objective of economic production is the enjoyment of the products. The individual engages in production in order to entitle himself to a share of the goods and services thus created (or to the equivalent of his share in purchasing power) which he wants for the use and enjoyment of himself and his dependents. He is not interested in toil per se. His concern is to legitimate his right to consume.

However, the production of wealth in the real world depends upon physical and technical factors. Universal capitalism, we must remember, begins with the proposition that there are two factors of production: the human factor (labor in all of its forms—intellectual and technical as well as manual), and the nonhuman factor (capital, defined as productive land, structures and machines). Although each factor produces wealth in exactly the same sense (physically, economically, politically and ethically), the part played by either in the productive process at any given moment and in each particular enterprise is determined by the current state and application of technology and by management practice.

Technology, the agent of economic change, is the process by which man harnesses nature *through his capital instru-*

ments and makes her work for him. Thus, technology acts
only upon the nonhuman factor of production. Its effect is
to increase the productiveness of capital at an accelerating
rate; that in turn paves the way for putting more of the nonhuman factor into production. Man himself remains
physically outside the process of technological change, his
innate capabilities no more altered by the invention of the
computer than by the steam engine or the wheel. The notion that technological change increases "human productivity" has no basis in fact; productively, man remains about
where history first found him. *Affluence, in short, is the
product of capital.*[27]

Economic employment (as distinguished from leisure
work, an end in itself) is simply a means to income. But
labor is only one factor of production, and it is not the one
that, beginning long before the industrial revolution, has
been increasing in productiveness. *If capital produces most
of the economy's wealth and income is distributed on the
basis of productive input, the individual can hardly reach
his goal—an affluent level of income—solely by means of
his labor.* Full employment is thus a deficient economic goal
if the function of an economy is to provide universal affluence, instead of universal busywork and equalized poverty.
Full employment, without simultaneous redistribution of
all the wealth or income produced by capital to noncapital-
owning employees, will never provide the fully employed
with sufficient purchasing power to buy all the goods and
services produced. If, on the other hand, it is accompanied
by such total redistribution, the social and political side
effects, and damage to incentive, condemn it on grounds
that have already been presented.

Finally, full employment is a socially hazardous goal. In
effect, it aspires to restore through political expedients the
pre-industrial state of toil that science, engineering, tech-

nology and modern management are pledged to overcome. Thus the political leadership finds its prestige contingent upon the success of an unnatural policy against which the most rational forces in the economy are aligned; a policy which it cannot enforce except at the cost of the demoralization and ultimately the destruction of the economy's productive sector. Desperation is inherent in that dilemma, and with it the temptation to use evil means. Thus the full-employment economy becomes increasingly prone to the worst of social evils: war and totalitarianism.

7 THE DISTRIBUTIVE PRINCIPLES OF VARIOUS SCHOOLS OF ECONOMIC THOUGHT

LAISSEZ-FAIRE ECONOMISTS pay lip service to capital as a factor of production, but they treat it functionally as something that mysteriously raises the "productivity" of labor. Therefore, the distributive principle of this school, while formally that of private property, in practice degenerates into needism. The concentration of capital ownership in a narrow segment of the population grows apace with technological advance. Government intervention to mitigate the effects of that concentration eventually becomes necessary to avert violent revolution. The theoretical weaknesses of classical economics assure that the inevitable governmental intervention will take a needist form.

Even though it formally advocates input as the distributive criterion, socialism is also compelled to practice the needist principle of distribution. Socialism holds that there is only one factor of production—labor. Its distributive rule is: "To each according to his labor." Whatever revolutionary purposes the labor theory of value may in their minds have served for the Marxists, in reality there are two factors of production. As technology shifts the effective burden of production from the human to the nonhuman factor, laboristic distributions become needist out of practical necessity. As under any other economic system, affluence (to the extent that a needist economy can achieve it) is the product of the nonhuman factor: capital. The capital is owned by the government, for the benefit of all citizens, it is claimed. But in practice the affluence capital produces is distributed by government office-holders. They have no choice but to base their distributive decisions on need, as they appraise it. No other course is open to them. Office-holders tend to decide that the most needy citizens in the economy, next to themselves, are their own families and friends, followed by those who manifest the most enthusiastic political support for the administration.

The Keynesians, formally committed to the classical and socialist goal of full employment, are as indifferent to distributive principle as they are to the idea of private property in any functional sense. They espouse many needist expedients because they believe that these will promote aggregate consumer demand and therefore full employment —the dearest goals of Keynesian economists. Their measures for improving the economic lot of individuals do not depend on any increase in the productive input of the individual; instead they are based on the need of the recipient for income, reinforced by the need of an economy always short (for reasons herein explained) of aggregate purchasing power and intent on seeking it through employment alone, or employment combined with welfare. No Keynesian has ever proposed a measure designed to make the *individual* more productive; for that would require institutional means for enabling him to acquire ownership of the nonhuman factor of production: capital.

Universal capitalism is based upon the private-property

principle of distributive justice. It may be summarized by rewording the traditional socialist principle to read: "From each according to what he produces, to each according to what he produces." Since universal capitalism holds that there are two factors of production, and that each produces wealth in the same physical, ethical, political and economic sense, it follows that an individual may produce through his labor, which he owns, or through his capital, which he owns, or through both. In either case, the rule of private property is applicable: "If you own it, you should get what it produces."

The very simplicity of the two-factor concept, when compared with the ponderous complexity of all preceding one-factor theories, can be misleading. It must be pointed out that the classical, the socialist, and the Keynesian schools have drawn their theoretical concepts largely from a world of symbolic logic: monetary theory. The theory of universal capitalism has its roots not in monetary theory, but in the real world of labor, natural resources, productive machines and devices of all sorts, technological and managerial know-how, engineering, and trade.[27a] It also has its root in anthropology, philosophy and the law, and in the psychology of private property from which political economy derives its political aspect. Universal capitalism is a realistic system that enables man to organize and carry out the production of goods and services he wants and needs, in a manner most compatible with his dual animal and spiritual nature and his physical constitution, while minimizing toil, maximizing leisure and respecting the natural right of equal economic opportunity for all men.

The theory of universal capitalism measures the adequacy of the legal, political and financial institutions that deal with economic activity, particularly those relating to the monetary system (through which value is measured and contractual arrangements are expressed) by how well those institutions serve desirable, real-world economic objectives that are physically and technologically feasible. The pragmatic emphasis here is quite the opposite of that employed by business under the tutelage of conventional schools of economic thought. The conventional approach puts the physical feasibility of an economic objective in second place. First consideration is given to the "financing" aspect. Only if the project can be "financed" under inflexible institutional arrangements that necessarily defeat the cause of general affluence is it undertaken.

Universal capitalism requires that the institutional arrangements (which we later discuss as the "invisible structure") be designed to accommodate objectives that are physically desired and physically feasible. Thus it makes institutions responsive to human requirements and the potential capability of the real world to satisfy those requirements.

8 THE CAUSE OF POVERTY

IN THE UNITED STATES today millions of families, politically described as affluent, are longing to triple and quadruple their present consumption on a qualitatively upgraded level, and millions more would like to get a toehold on the lower rungs the majority is straining to abandon. This consumer frustration takes place in an economy that possesses in abundance natural resources, manpower, entrepreneurial skills and highly productive capital instruments, together with the means for bringing about a vast increase in physical new capital formation. Indeed the frustration of the consumer, thwarted from acquiring the affluence he wants and needs, is matched only by the frustration of the producer, thwarted from expanding his output, a thing he could do with ease if only there were customers with ready cash or unsaturated credit. The problem is what it has always been in Western industrial society: poverty and semi-poverty in the midst of vast unused productive potential; as always, its cause is lack of purchasing power in the hands of those with economic wants and needs.

Why is it that millions of families find themselves unable to produce enough income to buy the things they desire— things not unreasonable in view of our industrial potential? If men vehemently detest being wards of charity, then

why the proliferation of schemes to cure poverty by redistributing income on the basis of need? The answer lies in
the relationships between people and the physical economy.
It lies in the technical facts of how wealth in a highly industrialized economy is produced—the facts as engineers
and cost accountants see them, not as those facts are interpreted by the denizens of the symbolic world of monetary
theory or by various needist politicians. For it is these
technical facts that necessarily determine the primary patterns of income distribution.

As there are only two factors of production—capital
and labor—all wealth is the product of one, the other, or
both. But the feature distinguishing an industrial economy
from the pre-industrial one from which it evolves is that
goods and services are increasingly the product of capital
instruments rather than human toil. The more technologically advanced the economy, the greater the input contribution of capital to total output, absolutely and proportion-
ately, for technology acts solely upon the nonhuman factor
in accordance with its logic, which is to shift the burden
of production from human beings to the forces of nature
harnessed through capital instruments.

In a private-property economy, the highly efficient capital instruments that are the source of the economy's affluence have owners. Owners are entitled to receive the wealth
their property produces, if the integrity of their private
property is not eroded. It is no more just to withhold the
earnings of capital from its owners than the earnings of
labor from its owners. But the owners of capital are (and
have always been) few, and capital is (as every working
man knows) the more productive factor. When accumulated
beyond a certain point, capital produces more income than
its owners can spend. There is nothing they can do with the
surplus except to invest it. The investment brings into being

new and more efficient capital instruments, which produce
an even greater income excess for their owners, who again
have no choice but to invest it. This process is endless,
cumulative and accelerating.

Production, however, implies consumption; mass production requires mass consumption. Although the purchasing power generated by a market economy is always
sufficient to buy the goods and services produced,[28] it cannot be used for that purpose unless it is in the pockets of
those having unfulfilled economic needs and wants. The
amount of purchasing power at the disposal of each household depends, in turn, on its productive contribution, i.e.,
large input, large outtake; small input, small outtake; no
input, no outtake.[29]

When capital instruments are responsible for most of
the productive input and they are narrowly held, the natural result is that a few families have purchasing power in
excess of their consumption needs, and the great majority
have needs in excess of their purchasing power. Since 2.3%
of American households own about 80% of the economy's
productive capital, and an additional 5 to 8% own the rest,[30]
the natural result is a shortage of the purchasing power
capable of sustaining affluence in most (90% or more)
American households. The shortage arises directly out of
the high concentration of ownership of the productive
power of capital.

If we stopped our analysis here, the institution responsible for the perennial imbalance between the industrial
power to produce and the economic power to consume
would certainly appear to be private property. Marx
thought so, and much of the world has come to believe him
right. But this conclusion, while credible, is false.[31] Private
property works like circuitry in electronics, or piping in
hydraulics. It conveys wages to the owners of labor power,

as well as the various forms of nonwage property income to the owners of capital. In itself, it is no more responsible for maldistribution of purchasing power than the science of bookkeeping is responsible for bankruptcy.

When capital owners are few, the private-property conduits of necessity create vast savings reservoirs for those few. If there were many owners, the same conduits would broadly irrigate the economy with purchasing power. It is not private property in itself that is economically harmful, but, rather, the fact that so few families own any significant amounts of it. Thus we must look *beyond* private property for the specific mechanism responsible for concentrating capital ownership. The cause, as Kelso and Adler have made clear, is the financing of new capital formation exclusively out of the accumulated financial savings of individuals and/ or their narrowly owned corporations.[32]

This hallowed old business custom insures that new capital will be owned by the person or corporation whose savings (assets) were used to finance it. Because the new capital is productive—otherwise there would have been no interest in bringing it into existence—it throws off its formation costs, with only rare exceptions, in a reasonably short time (usually less than five years) and then continues under normal depreciation policies to produce income for its owners for an indefinite period. The effect of the custom is (1) to give the owners of existing assets a monopoly of access to ownership of all the economy's future capital assets and, (2) to enable owners of pre-existing capital to pay for their acquisition of newly formed capital *out of the wealth produced by capital.* Thus, while distinct from private property, the capital-concentrating mechanism makes judicious use of that institution, and is so closely associated with it in everyday practice that even people closest to finance often do not yet see (or in any event, assiduously pretend not to see) that the two are functionally and logically separate.

As Harold Moulton of the Brookings Institution first pointed out in 1935, new capital does not have to be financed exclusively from past savings.[33] It can just as easily and logically be financed from credit, by means that create new capital owners simultaneously with new capital assets. Capital produces wealth. Unlike consumer goods, it is inherently financeable. With very slight alterations the same techniques being used today to finance the acquisition of non-income-producing consumer goods[34] can be employed (1) to vastly expand the existing economy—to build a Second Economy—and, (2) to enable noncapital-owning households to buy equity interests in new capital as it is formed, paying for it precisely as the capital owner (with rare exceptions) has always done—out of the income the newly formed capital produces.

All men have the right to participate in the production of wealth.[35] That is one of the three principles of economic justice;[36] it is implicit in the natural right to life. When wealth is produced primarily by the nonhuman factor, men must have the right to acquire viable amounts of capital as a supplement to their labor power. Economic opportunity in an industrial economy is not merely the opportunity to toil, but the opportunity *to own capital* and to acquire capital without having to invade the property of others, or to cut down on one's own already inadequate consumption.

To quote President Charles de Gaulle: "To stick to wages alone is to maintain a permanent class struggle."[36a]

PART II

The Second Income Plan

9 OBJECTIVES OF THE SECOND INCOME PLAN

EVEN A CASUAL READING of post-fifteenth-century history leaves no doubt about the primary motive power behind the conquest and industrialization of the North American continent. It was effective access to the private ownership of land, at that time the most important form of capital. Private ownership of land offered economic opportunity to the masses on a scale never seen in the world before or since. Certainly it was not the prospect of better poor laws that induced men and women to undergo the risk and travail that culminated in the thin layer of affluence now glittering on the pinnacle of our social structure.

The conquest of nature through the advance of technology, however, has evolved other forms of capital that have come to rival and even overshadow land in productive importance. It has been estimated that in 1964 the market value of total U.S. wealth was about 2.2 trillion dollars. Of this, land used in business and in agriculture comprised only ten percent, while the value of structures (i.e., land improvements) and other reproducible assets (capital instruments fabricated both by labor and by capital instruments) comprised more than 81%. Even after eliminating structures owned by the public, nonprofit and charitable institutions, nonrental real-estate improvements, and consumer durables, fabricated capital still comprised 38.3% of total wealth, or roughly four times the value of land used for productive purposes.[87]

As fabricated forms of capital have superseded land in productive importance in the American economy, no industrial counterpart to the open frontier or the Homestead Acts has been forthcoming. The modern world has no effective institutions for enabling men and women without accumulated savings to acquire ownership of the nonhuman factor of production, even though it is producing an ever-expanding portion of the economy's real wealth, making obsolete their labor. Unless such institutions are innovated, the tightly concentrated ownership of the existing economy must and will *defeat* the cause of general affluence.

In his study of *The Share of Top Wealth-Holders in National Wealth, 1922–1956,* Robert J. Lampman found no general change in the pattern of the concentrated ownership of capital between the 1920s and the 1950s.[88] He concluded that the 1.6% of the total adult population in 1953 who had $60,000 or more each in total assets, owned 82% of all corporate stock, virtually all state and local government bonds, and from 10 to 33% of each other type of property in the personal sector.[39] He further deduced that: "The association of high income and larger wealth-holding is also indicated by the concentration of property income in the higher income groups," and estimated that the top 1% of the adult population received 40% of the national total of property income.[40]

Let us be precise about the meaning of the word affluence. Affluence is the standard of living enjoyed by the top ten percent of the income pyramid, to the extent that such a standard *can* be achieved for all within the physical limits of available resources, manpower and know-how. It is our belief that in the United States, Canada and Mexico, and in most of the European and developing economies, general affluence is physically feasible within existing lifetimes —in the industrialized nations even within the lifetimes of those who are now middle-aged. It is elementary, however, that Canada and the United States would have to expand the productive capacity of their existing economies several times over in order to increase their present per capita output of goods and services to the level of general affluence. In less industrialized countries, where the affluent segment of the population is considerably narrower, the productive capacity of existing economies may have to be expanded fifteen, twenty or more times in order to build second economies capable of producing general affluence.

The Second Income Plan provides industry with the techniques for financing that gigantic expansion, while protecting and greatly strengthening the private ownership of existing capital against further redistributive erosion. At the same time it is designed to enable the noncapital-owning majority to buy, pay for, and thereafter own, in reasonable-sized holdings, the newly formed capital thus brought into existence. It is these new and expanded enterprises that comprise the second economy. Thus in the macrocosmic sense, the Second Income Plan is a method for building simultaneously (1) the industrial power of the people to produce wealth and therefore, (2) the legitimate power of the masses to consume it. The Plan supplies, in short, the missing piece of logic that industrial economies have been seeking almost from their beginning—the logic that can close the production-consumption gap—and in so doing, it puts within reach the most important of all economic goals.

10 THE INVISIBLE STRUCTURE

It may be easier to understand the Second Income Plan if we first recognize that each productive enterprise really consists of two separate structures. One is the physical structure that meets the eye. It may be land with a factory-building on it; the roads and railroads and utility lines that lead to and from it; the tools, equipment and machines that the physical structure contains; the trucks or other rolling stock that haul things back and forth, and the entire labor force that operates it. Or the physical structure may be a ship and its crew, and the docks at which it loads and unloads; perhaps a farm with its equipment, water, fertilizer, insecticide and pesticide sources, and its work force. The building and operation of this visible structure are the tasks of managers, engineers, technicians, accountants, lawyers, contractors, and clerical and operational workers.

Behind the physical structure, there is always an invisible structure made up of binding contractual commitments and ownership rights—a web of legal relationships. It is the invisible structure of enterprise that determines *who* participates in the process of production, and *who* by virtue of that participation is entitled to an income share from the proceeds of production. The invisible structure defines the relationships which all individuals who are in any way affected by the production process bear (1) to the two component physical factors (labor and capital) and, (2) to the distribution of the product or its value.

Chronologically, the invisible structure almost always precedes the physical structure to which it relates. This is so for a very simple reason. Those who participate in the production of wealth will not commit themselves until they know what they must contribute to the new enterprise, and what they will receive from it.[41]

A typical invisible structure may consist of a corporate charter and the corporate by-laws; the codes of positive law which give substance and sanction to the charter and by-laws; its effective "organization chart"; the decisions of the board of directors and officers who hold the offices provided for in the basic legal documents; the land and plant ownership documents; the contracts with officers and employees (including collective bargaining agreements); contractual arrangements with suppliers, distributors, and customers; the capital-stock-ownership arrangements with the "owners" of the corporation, the stockholders; and the financial contracts and arrangements with banks and others. The building and maintenance of the invisible structure of productive enterprise is the task of the entrepreneur, the manager, the labor leader, the lawyer, the banker, the investment banker, the accountant, and the owners of raw materials and other required physical capital.

All productive activity is a means to an end—human consumption and enjoyment. The goal of economic activity is the receipt, consumption and enjoyment of useful goods and services. Therefore, productive enterprise itself is only a means. Its visible structure is obviously necessary to produce goods and services, because they are material things. But its invisible structure is no less necessary, for it determines how the operations of the visible structure will affect

human beings, and indeed, whether there will even be a
visible structure. It is the invisible structure that connects
the visible structure of enterprise and its output with particular individuals. It is the invisible sector of the economy
(made up of all the invisible structures) that determines
whether all families and individuals within an economy
participate in the production of goods and services. The
combination of the physical quality and efficiency of the two
productive factors, labor and capital, and the content of the
invisible sector determine the extent of participation by
each individual or family.

If the invisible sector of the economy does not connect
particular families or individuals with its production processes, then the unconnected families or individuals will
neither participate in nor contribute to the economy's production of goods or services; nor will they *automatically,*
out of the process of production, receive a portion of the
wealth produced or the money-income representing it. The
significance of this is that they will have to satisfy their
creature comforts by means other than through participation in the productive process. In other words, their consumption will not be based upon productive input. It must
necessarily take the form of distribution on the basis of
need, from some part, or from all of the productive system.

Connecting nonproductive individuals with the visible
structure in a manner that enables them to receive economic outtake transforms the invisible structure into a redistributive device for taking from the productive and giving to the unproductive. It ruptures the property relations
of the invisible structure. It is not a method for enabling
more persons to contribute input as a condition to being
entitled to outtake.

Production of goods and services is a physical activity.
To connect an individual with enterprise in such manner

that he receives a distributive share without making a physical, i.e., *physically effective*, contribution to production, is simply a method of distributing the output to the nonproductive without increasing it. For example, to pay unemployment compensation to individuals, or to pay them a guaranteed annual income, or to make payments to them in the form of negative income-tax distributions, or to pay them for featherbedding, is, in each instance, to divide the product of the economy without increasing it.

If it is possible, through the accepted workings of an economy, to acquire wealth without (1) producing it, (2) owning something that increases in market value or, (3) being the beneficiary of a voluntary gift, the organization of the invisible structure is *per se* defective. It is not designed to keep just accounts between the individuals engaging in production and consumption, but to facilitate fraud and theft. "If you want to make money, don't horse around with steel or lightglobes. Go where the money is —in the money business," advised the founder of a half-billion-dollar mutual fund established in Geneva in order to evade income taxes for its international clients.[42] But real wealth *is* steel and lightglobes and other mundane tangibles produced by the visible structure. The invisible sector produces no wealth, but if it contains defects, it may and often does enable those who produce no wealth to acquire it.

There are only two factors of production: the human factor, labor, and the nonhuman factor, capital. One who owns neither the productive labor power nor the productive capital required in the process of production cannot make a physical contribution to the production of real wealth. Under those circumstances the receipt of a distributive share is obviously unjust. It hurts the human dignity of the recipient and demotivates those who have produced the product. Its economic effect is to equalize poverty rather than to enable affluence to be universally produced, distributed and enjoyed.

The proposals of the Second Income Plan are based upon the concepts of universal capitalism and its private-property principle of distribution; the latter implying that affluent levels of income for families and individuals are a function of high levels of productive input into the economy.

Proposals affecting the visible structure are designed to bring about rapid economic growth—the building of a second economy large enough to produce affluence for all, in a time short enough to benefit generations now living. While the term *second economy* is a synonym for economic expansion, it must not be confused with the simple enlargement of the gross national product proposed by advocates of needist growthmanship.

11 THE DESIGN OF THE INVISIBLE SECTOR UNDER THE SECOND INCOME PLAN

LET US FIRST TURN our attention to the visible structure of enterprise. The physical prerequisites to the production of general affluence are (1) natural resources, aside from mere land, available in adequate quantities from domestic or other sources, including the means of producing power; (2) adequately trained or trainable labor power, including managerial labor power; (3) the nonhuman factor of production, i.e., land, structures, and machines; (4) access to productive know-how, including the technical knowledge of how to produce machines, devices, structures, etc.; (5) physical need not already satisfied, combined with the general desire for satisfaction.

The United States, Canada, Mexico, most European economies, Great Britain, Japan, and most of the developing economies either already possess, or through established trade channels have access to, all the physical requisites for the production of general affluence. If this is so, why then don't these countries produce general affluence for the people who live in them?[43] Why is there found in each one, including the United States (in terms of *general affluence*, 90% underdeveloped), a pyramid-shaped social structure composed of increasingly impoverished layers of population, viewed downward towards the base, with the apex crowned by a few affluent families?[44]

We submit that the responsibility rests with the primitive state of our knowledge of economics. Our minds are still dominated by pre-industrial attitudes and habits of thought, all of which are focused on *one* of the factors of production, rather than upon both. Like the denizens of Plato's cave, we are preoccupied with the monetary shadows of reality, rather than reality itself.

This assertion should not be taken lightly. The wide discrepancies between the solutions to economic problems arrived at through monetary thinking and their real-life results, in terms of enabling people peacefully and rationally to produce and consume general affluence, must be attributed to the ease with which symbols are confused with the physical realities for which they stand. Money is not a part of the visible sector of the economy; people do not consume money. Money is not a physical factor of production, but rather a yardstick for measuring economic input, economic outtake and the relative values of the real goods and services of the economic world. Money provides a method of measuring obligations, rights, powers and privileges. It provides a means whereby certain individuals can accumulate claims against others, or against the economy as a whole, or against many economies. It is a system of symbols that many economists substitute for the visible sector and its productive enterprises, goods and services, thereby losing sight of the fact that a monetary system is a part only of the invisible sector of the economy, and that its adequacy can *only* be measured by its effect upon the visible sector.

Since the production and consumption of goods and services are physical activities, they relate to the visible sector of the economy. Thus the question of whether the economy can produce sufficient goods and services to achieve general affluence should not be initially addressed to the men who concern themselves with the invisible structure. It first should be addressed to owners of resources, the workers, managers, engineers, scientists and technicians. Decisions relating to *physical* feasibility are not the concern of economists, lawyers, politicians, bankers or investment bankers. These latter have no function except to design and organize the invisible structure in such a manner that those who are to consume affluence (i.e., all households and individuals) become the producers of affluence, because in the incentive society—the private-property economy which alone is capable of producing general affluence—only those who produce affluence may enjoy it. The work of the fabricators of the invisible structure must be judged solely in terms of whether a gross national product commensurate with the general affluence the economy is physically capable of producing is (1) in fact produced and, (2) produced through the viable participation of *all* households in the economy. To the extent that a particular family cannot, due to the state of technology, make a contribution to production through its labor input great enough to entitle it to affluence, the family must be enabled by the *invisible* structure to make up for this deficiency through capital input. In summary:

(1) The physical means of producing general affluence exist.

(2) There are but *two* factors of production.

(3) A high level of productive input by each family will entitle it to an affluent distributive share of income.

When, under circumstances that are physically feasible, citizens of the United States ask where they are going to get the "money" to eliminate poverty from the central cities, or from Appalachia, or from the Mississippi Delta, or Canadians ask how they can develop the potash deposits of Saskatchewan without U.S. "money," it is because they do not understand how affluence is produced in an industrial economy. Otherwise they would reject the questions as irrelevant. They are measuring the feasibility of activity in the real world by the adequacy of the invisible sector. They are treating the invisible sector, which is institutional in character, as if it were the actual enterprises it represents. They do not understand that the adequacy of the symbols used by the invisible structure depends solely upon the performance of the visible structure. In other words, it is not money that produces goods and services, but rather *the sufficiency of the money and credit system that is measured by its effectiveness in facilitating physically feasible economic activity.*

Anyone who has trouble understanding the distinction between money and goods and services might do well to reread the Greek legend of King Midas, whom Bacchus granted the power of changing whatever he might touch into gold. But to Midas' dismay, bread hardened in his hand; morsels of food defied his teeth; and wine turned to liquid gold in his throat. The relationship between money and goods and services is even clearer if we substitute for the gold of the Midas legend, paper money, or IBM symbols on a readout tape.[45]

Monetary thinking, because it is symbolic, can never be used to justify or verify itself; its adequacy must be constantly tested against the real world of physical goods and services, in relation to the physical desire of people for goods and services. This means that the adequacy of the invisible sector must always be checked against the physical reality of the visible sector, as a map is constantly checked against the physical terrain it is intended to describe.

Private property relates input directly to outtake. When the money and credit system enables certain inhabitants of the economy to enjoy outtake without input, or to receive disproportionately large outtake in relation to input, it is the money and credit system that fails to conform to the law of property or the private-property principle of distribution. What is presumably legitimate in the shadow-world of monetary and financial thinking is fraud and injustice in the world of real-life economics. This fraud and injustice can only be discovered, understood and corrected by understanding that the validity of monetary and financial thinking, as in the case of the invisible sector as a whole, must always be tested against the physical reality of the visible sector, and not the other way around.

If it is man's nature to feel that he can legitimately consume in the economic order only what he himself has produced (with exceptions not here relevant), and if the monetary and financial design of the invisible structure of an economy having the physical potential for affluence disqualifies most men from becoming productive at affluent levels, then the monetary and financial thinking is defective. It is defective because it does not provide an effective invisible structure to enable the visible sector to accomplish its desirable and feasible goal.

One of the virtues of the Second Income Plan is that its invisible structure is consistent with the physical and productive goals of universal capitalism, and also with its ethical assumptions. Thus the financial and monetary measures that make up the Second Income Plan are consistent with the goal of general affluence with a minimum of toil, with the concept of economic justice, and with the hatred of parasitism that seems implicit in man's nature. In other words, the institutional arrangements of the Second Income Plan have been made deliberately subordinate to the physical world and responsive to its requirements. These institutional arrangements are internally consistent. Attempts to discredit Second Income Plan financing techniques because they do not conform to the preconceptions of conventional financing techniques, when these have already demonstrated their practical inadequacy, should be regarded as irrelevant.

12 THE BACKGROUND OF THE SECOND INCOME PLAN

THE FOLLOWING is a summary of the theoretical considerations which dictate the design of the tools for implementing the Second Income Plan:

(1) Capital, the nonhuman factor of production, is the predominant source of affluence in any free economy.

(2) Capital (the nonhuman factor) and labor (the human factor) are separate and readily identifiable factors of production, each producing or contributing to the production of economic goods or services. In reality the presence of the nonhuman factor in any form does not make the human factor more productive: it makes the combination more productive. If the price of both factors in this competition for the opportunity to produce is determined in reasonably competitive markets, in most instances (as Karl Marx unhappily observed) the value of the human factor is reduced. The "productivity" of labor (if cleverly defined as *unit output per hour of the combination*) may go up. But the value of the productive input of labor, the basis of its compensation under competitive conditions, goes down if the principle of distribution employed is that based on input: the private-property principle.

(3) The economic function of technology is to harness nature through the nonhuman factor of production and to make her produce affluence for men.

(4) The most effective motivational arrangement known to man is for each individual to be protected in the receipt and enjoyment of what he produces through his labor, through his capital, or through both.

(5) It is just as moral for an individual to produce the wealth he desires to consume through his privately owned capital as through his privately owned labor power.

(6) In a market economy, the purchasing power created in the process of production is equal to the market value of goods and services produced. This is simply double-entry bookkeeping. Thus, the *aggregate* purchasing power is always adequate to enable people with unsatisfied needs and wants to consume the output of the economy.[46] However, it would be a mistake to assume, as did several early laissez-faire economists, that *potentially* adequate purchasing power will actually be used to purchase the economy's output. Goods and services will be removed from the market only if those who have unsatisfied economic wants and needs are the persons who produce the economy's wealth. For only the producers, under a private-property economy, receive the resultant purchasing power. As economies are now structured, the opportunity to produce wealth has no necessary relation to the individual's or household's desire or need to consume wealth; nor is there any way under one-factor economic concepts to put in proportion these two equally vital and interdependent functions.

(7) Mass consumption (e.g., general affluence) is necessary to support mass production, and vice versa.

(8) Equality of economic opportunity, i.e., opportunity to produce affluence, cannot be satisfied by mere opportunity to be employed when capital already produces most of

the wealth and will produce progressively more of it each year.

(9) New capital formation in well-managed businesses (e.g., the top 2,000 U.S. corporations) does not come into existence unless it will pay for itself in a reasonably short period of time—generally under five years. One of the key responsibilities of management is the enforcement of this rule. *Newly formed capital is therefore inherently finance-able.* Capital normally pays its costs of formation and then continues to produce goods or services for an indefinite period, its productiveness preserved both by physical main-tenance and by accounting, depreciation and amortization procedures. Well-managed businesses rigidly subject the nonhuman factor to "birth control." The human factor, by contrast, comes into existence without reference to the economy's physical need for labor.

(10) Contrary to what lending institutions of all kinds encourage us to believe, the purchasing power of the con-sumer is not increased by consumer credit. Consumer goods purchased on credit increase neither the buyer's income nor his productive power; on the contrary, interest costs—some-times as high as 18% per annum in the consumer-goods field —decrease the effective purchasing power of his income to buy useful goods and services. *Consumer goods are thus inherently non-financeable.* They do not pay their costs of acquisition. They do not produce wealth or income after they have been acquired.

(11) The common characteristic of all industrial eco-nomies whose invisible sectors are not structured in accord-ance with the theory of universal capitalism is that they tend to produce more than they can consume. Their pro-ductive potential in the form of newly formed capital that could physically be brought into existence is vastly greater than the economic power to consume of the masses with un-

satisfied needs and wants. It is obviously easier for the free industrial economies, using one-factor economic concepts, to solve their physical problems of production than their problems of enabling those with unsatisfied wants and needs to participate in production to an extent sufficient to provide them automatically with adequate purchasing power. Automation tends to intensify this difficulty.

(12) The redistribution of purchasing power from the highly productive to the less productive or nonproductive, whatever needist device is used to accomplish the task, is a primary source of social strife. The economically productive resent being relieved of their wealth. The underproductive resent having their needs and wants satisfied as wards of charity; nor can any amount of rhetorical sophistry deceive either party about the truth. Needist redistribution is better than violent revolution, but it is an expedient of last resort; it is not the answer to the question of how an economy either can or should achieve general affluence.

Failure of so-called modern political-economic theories to take into account these basic truths has deprived the United States and other economies of the world of rational economic systems capable of producing and, through general participation in the productive process, automatically distributing general affluence.

In the United States, in most of the other Western economies, and in Japan, minor changes in the invisible sectors of these economies would provide the institutional framework which would enable them to produce and distribute general affluence in accordance with their physical capacities, both existing and potential, to do so. Minor reforms can create the conditions necessary to liberate the enormous and unique motivational power inherent in the human instinct to acquire and to own a viable and defendable interest in those external things which are the sources of his economic well-being. Such reforms gradually can eliminate the social strife engendered by redistribution, whether it is expressed through union or other coercion, or through fraud, theft, riot, or anarchy.

A rapidly expanding economy structured to provide genuine equality of economic opportunity to all of its households can gradually dispense with needist expedients.

13 THE PRACTICAL MEASURES

CLEARLY A DESIRABLE (though not indispensable) first step for any economy is the adoption of a sound national economic goal.[47] In the United States our present goal is contained in the Employment Act of 1946, an admirable document in that it recognizes the right of all Americans to be economically productive, but pre-industrial in that it equates productiveness only with human toil. The same flaw vitiates the Economic Opportunity Act of 1964. There, economic opportunity for the nonpropertied is defined strictly in terms of toil, and much of the great body of economic legislation between 1932 and the present is based on the same backward and unrealistic premise. In a nation that calls itself capitalist, there is no recognition, either official or unofficial, that capital ownership should be a legitimate goal for all Americans.

Any reader who doubts the truth of this statement is invited to search the Employment Act of 1946 and the various hearings and reports that led to its enactment; the hearings, staff reports, and monologues of the Temporary National Economic Committee, 1938–41; *Goals for Americans,* the report of the President's Commission on National Goals, 1960; *Prospect for America,* the Rockefeller Panel reports, 1961; the reports of the Commission on Money and Credit,

1963; the report of the National Commission on Technology, Automation, and Economic Progress, 1966; the numerous hearings and staff reports of the Joint Economic Committee relating to national economic policy; and reports of the Council of Economic Advisers dealing with the impact of technology on the American economy. In each of these studies and reports the necessity for a deliberate and systematic broadening of capital ownership would seem to be of the most vital importance—indeed, to constitute the heart of the matter. Yet the subject is not so much as raised. Even the Invest in America Committee, organized by groups within the United States "securities industry," can only be said to promote the reshuffling of outstanding securities, primarily among financial intermediaries and among the top ten percent of wealth holders. Its program neither contains nor contemplates the sharp tools of the Second Income Plan for (1) building the second economy, and (2) enabling families without savings to buy equities newly issued in the course of building the second economy, paying for them out of income produced by the resulting new physical capital.

Upon asking economists, authors, foundation officials, philanthropists, and others connected with the above-mentioned studies of economic goals why the various studies failed to recognize capital ownership for all families and individuals as a desirable economic goal, we found their responses quite uniform. After an initial period of astonishment and confusion that anyone should raise such a question, they vigorously asserted that of course capital ownership *is* a desirable goal for every family and individual in every economy. Upon hearing our suggestions as to how this could be accomplished, and how, in certain instances for which we are partly responsible, it *is* being accomplished, they uniformly replied that they had "serious doubts" about the *means* we suggest. Following the questioning, varying periods of months or years elapsed, and, although on record as to how very important it is for every society to have sound economic goals, for the U.S. economic goal to include broad capital ownership, and for the society's leadership to work for the achievement of such goals, the individuals who were questioned unanimously dropped the subject of capital ownership for the masses. None of them corrected their acknowledged omission to recognize capital ownership for all as a proper economic goal, and none of them instituted studies to ascertain the *proper* means—if our proposals are not proper means—for accomplishing this goal, or to allay their doubts about the propriety of the means we suggest. All remained in positions of leadership responsibility where economic goals and their pursuit continued to be an admitted field of interest.

Different persons will undoubtedly draw different conclusions from these experiences, but our conclusions are: (1) The psychology which underlies the *means test* in the needist welfare programs also underlies the thinking of the owners of concentrated capital when they concern themselves about the economic problems of the masses, or when "experts" under their influence prepare studies in that field. Their concern is with the temporary elimination of the effects (and superficial appearances) of poverty, not the creation of general affluence. Even where it is clear to them that the creation of general affluence is feasible and that it would not diminish their own affluence in any way but, rather, would bulwark and fortify it, unconsciously they enjoy—and are in a position to enjoy—the distinction between an economy that fights poverty and one that rationally sets about to create the conditions of general affluence. (2) The first move, the initiative, in the creation of general affluence must come from those who do not have it. Fortunately, this is neither a small nor a powerless group, for, in addition to labor in general, and minority races in general, it also includes corporate middle management, a large slice of top management, educators, civil servants, legislators, judges, scientists, most engineers, most lawyers, most accountants, artists, writers, and social scientists. The conspiracy of silence that suppresses recognition of the necessity of capital ownership for all families and individuals as indispensable goals of a generally affluent economy, and suppresses the debate and experiments so urgently needed to develop effective means for achieving that goal, is supported by an extremely small but strategically placed group of people. Once the concept of universal capitalism becomes generally known, once the idea of capital ownership becomes integrated into the idea of equality of economic opportunity, the conspiracy—with the silence—will vanish.[48]

What is required in the United States is policy legislation: a Full Production Act, to be enacted by Congress, acknowledging the economic responsibility of business, labor unions and government to enable all Americans to participate fully in the economy and to produce affluence—through their labor, to the extent that labor is necessary under prevailing technology, and through capital ownership, to the extent that goods and services comprising affluence are the product of capital. Since the capital-labor input ratio is already high and increases progressively with the advancing frontiers and application of technology, the legislation should also authorize the research necessary to carry out the Act's objectives.[49] Statistics on the nation's progress in expanding its proprietary base should be included in the President's Annual Economic Report. The Act might well establish a special cabinet post to administer this new responsibility. Having a secretary of capital ownership makes at least as much sense as a secretary of labor, and in an industrial economy, rather more.[50] A proposed text for such policy legislation, written in the style of the Employment Act of 1946, is set forth in the Appendix as "The Full Production Act of 19——."

The objective of the Second Income Plan, as we stated earlier, is the building of the second economy—an economy that, in the United States, must have several times the per capita productive power of the existing one. The means of accomplishing that physical objective (changes in the invisible structure of industry and business) must be so designed that the Second Economy will be owned primarily by the 90% of families and individuals who do not own viable holdings of productive capital today. These new capital-owning families can then engage in the production of wealth both through their employment (to the extent required by the current state of technology) and through their capital ownership. Our proposed tools relate to the following areas of the invisible sector:

(1) Estate planning and the pattern of testamentary and intervivos gifts as they are affected by national and state tax policy.

(2) The conduct of the corporation and the design of corporate strategy.

(3) Financing capital ownership for corporate employees.

(4) Financing capital ownership for noncorporate employees.

14 TAX POLICY CHANGES AFFECTING ESTATE AND GIFT TAXATION AND ESTATE PLANNING

ALTHOUGH SECOND INCOME PLAN tax policy as it affects estates and gifts is a book-length subject, the basic policy changes needed primarily and initially at the federal or national level can be briefly summarized.

Federal estate and gift taxation in the United States and Canada provides a very minor source of revenue. It has the effect, however, of driving the capital of large estates into tax-exempt foundations. Capital thus impounded can no longer serve the purpose that the nonhuman factor must serve in a private property economy.

When capital is transferred from individual ownership to foundation ownership, the invisible structure of enterprise in which the foundation owns securities ceases to connect productive capital and the benefits of its ownership with individuals. As a factor of production, capital so diverted becomes *nonpeople connected*. In effect, the capital becomes owned by the government. The wealth it produces

can no longer be used for the benefit of individuals, but
only for "public purposes" as they are determined by the
ruling bureaucracy. On the one hand, individuals who
might otherwise acquire the ownership of such capital are
deprived of the economic opportunity it could provide
them to make a productive contribution to the economy.
On the other hand, the ever-present inadequacy of the purchasing power of individuals to consume the wealth that
is produced or potentially (but for the purchasing power
deficiency) *could* be produced, is aggravated.

While the economy might, for good and sufficient reasons, continue to maintain the tax-exempt status of traditional religious, educational and hospital institutions, the
general-purpose foundation is a dangerous rupture in the
connection between one of the two factors of production
and the great number of individuals who, without it, can
never be productive enough legitimately to enjoy affluence.
Capital is a factor of production. It is just as critical that it be
coupled in reasonable sized holdings with individuals, who
thereby are enabled to become both producers (or more
productive) and consumers (or more affluent consumers),
as it is that labor power be privately owned by individuals.
The transfer of capital ownership to large general-purpose
foundations destroys the possibility of such individual relationship.

Not only is the concentration of philanthropy in the
hands of the few a social evil, but, because the ownership-
concentration process on which it rests is a direct cause
of the nonownership of capital by millions of families, it is
one cause of the evil of poverty to which philanthropy
(sometimes) addresses itself. It is, in short, an arrangement
which prevents millions of families from becoming more
productive through their capital ownership. It contributes
to needist redistribution of the concentrated holdings of

capital, both before capital is trapped in foundations and afterwards.

Since it is impossible for owners of large capital estates to take their wealth with them when they go, it is vital, and certainly it is a proper concern of social policy, that they should leave their large holdings here on earth under arrangements which promote the peaceful functioning of economies and the advance of civilization towards individual autonomy, personal affluence, leisure, and the highest forms of creative work. Specifically, we would suggest modification of the tax laws to permit the wealthy, in various ways, to leave their wealth to individuals selected by them, *tax free,* as they now can to exempt foundations, providing that safeguards are imposed to prevent particular recipients from acquiring excessively large holdings in that manner. For example, tax-exempt gifts by individuals to employee deferred-benefit trusts should be permitted. Similarly, tax-exempt gifts to individuals, whether related by blood or marriage or not, should be permitted, with a steeply graduated tax to apply if the capital estate of the recipient, *after receipt of the gift,* exceeds some legislatively defined viable capital holding.

We estimate that more than one million new viable capital estates per year could be created through this single measure alone, thus enabling over a million more families each year to increase their affluence-producing power through capital ownership.

15 PROPOSALS RELATING TO THE CONDUCT OF THE CORPORATION

THAT IT IS NOW "easy" in industrialized economies, as C.P. Snow and others have observed, spectacularly to increase the output of goods and services, is due in large measure to one of man's most useful and beneficial inventions: the corporation. The unique power of the corporation to marshal the two factors of production, capital and labor, into enterprises capable of producing efficiently the almost infinite variety of goods and services desired by consumers and industry has been justly celebrated. The superiority of the corporate structure over other forms of organization is demonstrated by the fact that the corporation is the dominant building block of the invisible structures of all non-socialized industrial economies (which is to say, the most successful of the industrial economies). In the United States, for example, corporations own more than 70% of the economy's productive capital and turn out about the same percentage of total goods and services.

But the functional perfection of which the corporation is capable will be fully revealed only to the society that first structures its economy on the principles of universal capitalism and the Second Income Plan. As that society will quickly discover, the corporation is ideally suited to eliminate the distribution bottleneck in the advanced industrial nations, and to keep the bottleneck from arising in nations in the process of industrializing. In the former, the problem is one of enabling the nonaffluent masses to consume the high output its corporations could produce if only there were adequate economic demand. In the latter, the problem is one of discovering new patterns of development that simultaneously build the industrial power to produce goods and services and the economic power of the people to consume them, and to maintain the balance between these equally vital economic forces until a production-consumption level is reached that is consistent with the sustained enjoyment of general affluence.

The modern corporation is the perfect device for connecting the productive power of the nonhuman factor of production, capital, with *individual persons* through their property rights as stockholders. It is the perfect device for subjecting the individual with no capital to a form of benign coercion, through which he can painlessly become the owner of *future savings*. The corporation can be used to enable the individual to buy capital ownership and pay for it out of the wealth produced by that capital, so that his current levels of consumption from current income remain unimpaired. In brief, the corporation properly utilized has an almost magical power to answer two of the most critical questions of our time, namely, (1) how can the propertyless individual acquire ownership of productive capital and, (2) how can we structure the economy so that the power of the people as a whole to buy goods and services grows in step with expanding productive power?

The efficacy of the corporation to connect *people* with the productive power of capital has always been known to a few persons; unfortunately, they have been content to keep the knowledge to themselves. Exclusive use of the power of the corporation by the few has converted a potentially great human and social blessing into an intolerable economic blight.

Thus far in history, the corporation has served as an instrument for connecting the tiny capital-owning minority with productive power so vast that it exceeds their physical capacity or desire to consume. "Your fortune is rolling up, rolling up like an avalanche. You must keep up with it. You must distribute it faster than it grows. If you do not, it will crush you, and your children and your children's children," a friend advised John D. Rockefeller over a half-century ago.[51] A party J. Paul Getty gave at his Sutton Place residence in London in July of 1960, attended by more than 1,000 distinguished guests, was described by the *London Daily Express* as "easily the most fabulous evening since the war." During eight hours of concerted and experienced spending, it was estimated that Mr. Getty succeeded in disposing of about $30,000 of purchasing power. During the same eight-hour period, however, the *Express* estimated (and almost certainly underestimated) that his capital produced for him $67,000![52]

At that point, as we have already shown, sheer human necessity compels the economically disfranchised to use their organized power blocs, and government itself, to redistribute either the real wealth, or the purchasing power which it represents, from those who produce more than they can consume to those who need or desire to consume more than they can produce. Minor changes in the corporation and in the tax laws prevailing in most countries can correct the ancient misuse of the corporation, and transform it into an instrument which serves the *many* instead of the few.

Up to this stage in history, corporate strategy has consisted entirely of ideas on how to maximize output, minimize cost, and maximize profit. But since output has no rational ultimate purpose except to satisfy the consumer needs of individuals, the traditional goals of the corporation are insufficient and incomplete. In preoccupying itself only with the production of goods and services, while remaining oblivious to its unique ability and obligation to build the power of the masses to buy its output, corporate management has been blind to its opportunity for assuming (and properly so) a major share of the society's socioeconomic planning. Management has unknowingly delegated one of its most vital (and most interesting) responsibilities to government and to various government-supported power blocs.[53]

Practical implementation of an economy structured along the lines of universal capitalism begins with corporate management. The first step is recognition by management that it has both the opportunity and the duty to use its own prerogatives and the production-marshalling efficacy of the corporation to connect individual consumers with the productive power of the corporation, either through employment, to the degree that the state of technology requires participation by labor, or through the ownership of the non-human factor of production represented by the capital of the corporation itself. Once corporate management broadens its thinking to include intelligent concern for the consumer's power to buy as well as for production, once management realizes that as new productive power is built, it must be linked with individual consumers who will use it to consume, and that it is management's own responsibility to see that it never builds productive power without making a corresponding increase in the power of financially underpowered individuals to buy the corporation's output, the simple legislative changes needed at the national and local levels of government can be easily achieved.

One of the first legislative reforms required is a gradual

step-by-step elimination of the corporate income tax. Some of the most important methods of implementing the Second Income Plan involve the financing of capital ownership for individuals without savings by enabling them to buy and pay for their holdings entirely out of the income the newly created capital instruments produce. Those methods would be blunted by taxes (state and federal) that (in the United States economy) divert to government more than half of the income produced by capital. The pre-tax profitability of major U.S. nonfinancial corporations reviewed annually in the April *Monthly Economic Letter* of the First National City Bank of New York (after all the artful concealment of profits of which modern corporate accounting is capable) exceeds 20% of book net worth, and in many cases is closer to 30%. And this computation does not reflect the enormous redistribution from the stockholders to the workers, both directly and indirectly (as where non-union employee compensation is raised to match union gains or to prevent unionization) which takes place within the corporation through coercive bargaining.

Now we come to a remarkable paradox and a fact that is not generally known, or even suspected by the public at large. Although the corporate income tax falls entirely upon the wealth produced by capital (after all labor costs have been discharged), and although, as we have noted, ownership of productive capital is highly concentrated, with all of it lying within the top ten percent of wealthholders, and the great bulk within the top one percent of wealthholders, it is not the concentrated wealthholder that the corporate income tax hurts most. True, if the corporate income tax did not rupture the property channel of the invisible structure of enterprise in the United States, far more than twice as much capital-produced income would be available for distribution to the small class of capital owners. But even if that income were distributed (and there is no assurance that the corporations would distribute it, for reasons to be explained later in this chapter), the ability of the top wealthholders to enjoy affluence would not be much increased, if any.

There are limits to the amount of wealth one can respectably consume in an economy where the majority of families are nonaffluent or simply poor. Top wealthholders have long since reached that limit. Thus full payout of all the income produced by capital would simply accelerate further the investment spiral, and concentrate capital ownership even more solidly. The top wealthholders can well afford the 50% erosion of their property in capital which is accomplished by the corporate income tax. The mechanics of conventional business finance are working to aggrandize their capital holdings faster than the forces of needist redistribution can erode them away. *It is the capitalless masses, who never will be able to acquire capital legitimately unless they can buy and pay for it out of the wealth it produces, who cannot afford to have ownership invaded to any degree.*

Secondly, we propose that each mature corporation (defined as a corporation that has effective access to market sources of capital funds, including funds available under Second Income Plan proposals to finance new capital formation[53a]) must gradually be compelled, by tax guidance, amendment of relevant corporation laws, or otherwise, to pay out all of its net earnings, after depreciation and operating reserves only, to its stockholders. The right of the owner —the stockholder—to receive all the net income produced by what is owned is the essence of private property. To withhold the wages of capital is no more justifiable than to withhold the wages of labor. Stated affirmatively, the flow of purchasing power to those who engage in producing wealth

is just as disrupted by corporate management's withholding
the wages of capital (corporate net earnings) as it would be
were the wages of labor withheld.

Like the corporate income tax, the practice of corporate
boards of directors to withhold from stockholders the income their capital produces (retained earnings) does not
hurt primarily the concentrated wealthholder. It hurts the
small capitalist, who needs his dividends to live on, and
it hurts the individual who owns no capital at all, but who
could become an owner under the techniques of the Second
Income Plan. If non-capital-owning households and individuals are to be enabled to buy and pay for capital out
of its earnings—and this, let us repeat, is their only hope
of ever acquiring capital ownership by legitimate means—
it is crucial that they receive those earnings in full.

Retention of earnings gives rise to the same strange
paradox as the corporate income tax. Under our ill-conceived scheme of tax laws, the owner of a larger capital
estate can actually save taxes by corporate withholding of
earnings. He is thus enabled to convert income taxable in
high brackets (up to 70%) into capital gains, taxable in
low brackets (not over 25%), or into appreciated assets held
for investment and not taxed at all! Not only can members
of the small affluent class afford arbitrary retention of corporate earnings, the practice actually works to their advantage.
But it devastates the hopes of all those who can acquire
affluence only through financed acquisition of newly issued
capital equities.

Clearly, the elimination of the corporate income tax,
thus shifting the revenue-raising burden of government to
the ultimate taxpayers—the individual citizens—where it
belongs, combined with the forcing of corporations to pay
their net earnings to those who own the corporate capital—
the stockholders—will enormously increase the financeabil-

ity of newly issued corporate equities by the nonaffluent. Both measures will, of course, also necessitate the scaling down of the personal income tax. Otherwise, excessive revenues would be raised by government from individuals in tax brackets higher than the corporate income tax (presently 48% in the U.S. at the federal level).

Thirdly, we must provide the corporation with a new and unlimited source for financing its growth, to replace the internally generated funds which today finance the growth of most of the Western world's business corporations. It is this internal financing of corporate new capital formation that is the most effective wealth-concentrating mechanism. In the United States, for example, all but five percent of new capital formation is now internally financed; thus a stationary ownership base is assured. Of the five percent that is not internally financed, four and a half percent is financed through debt securities that must be repaid from internally generated cash flow, and the remaining half of one percent is equity stocks, mostly of public utilities that are *forced* by their regulatory agencies to finance their growth partially through the sale of equities.[54]

The Second Income Plan provides the corporation with two alternate sources for financing its new capital formation. The first is a form of employee deferred-compensation plan which we call the Second Income Plan Trust. It enables corporate employees to purchase newly issued corporate equities *on pre-tax corporate earnings*. The second is the Financed Capitalist Plan for enabling noncorporate employees to purchase newly issued corporate equities, and to pay for them out of the *pre-tax earnings* of the corporate equities so purchased. Both proposals will be discussed in the following chapters.

Both plans embody the logical symmetry characteristic of proposals making up the Second Income Plan. It is no secret that in none of the economies of the world can the goal of affluence for every family be achieved without an enormous expansion of productive enterprise; in particular, without a massive expansion of new capital formation. Thus, on the one hand, the majority of families in each of these economies, if they are to have the opportunity to produce affluence to enjoy thereby its consumption, must become the owners of productive capital. They must do so in order to increase their productive input. On the other hand, corporate enterprises, which produce the bulk of the goods and services of industrial economies, must have an infinitely expandable source of financing for their acquisition of new plant and equipment. This is a prerequisite for creating a second economy capable of producing general affluence.

Those equal and reciprocal requirements have always existed, but to date, all concepts of corporate strategy, except one built upon the theory of universal capitalism and the Second Income Plan, have failed to provide for them. In general, there is no recognition of the fact that in failing to plan the great expansions of corporate productive capital, upon which the affluence-producing capacity of industrial economies must be built, in ways which enable millions of new families to buy, pay for, and employ capital ownership in their lives, management is spearheading the destruction of private property in the nonhuman factor of production and is forcing governments around the world increasingly to employ needist redistributive measures in order to fill the growing purchasing-power gap.

Corporate management, in short, is preoccupied with only half of what could be considered a valid strategy; it is seeking vigorously to build the industrial power to produce affluence, but failing miserably in expanding the *productive power* of consumers (and thereby automatically expanding their consumer purchasing power) through extending to them the opportunity to buy, pay for, and own productive capital equities. Through that defective strategy, management is abdicating its responsibility under a private-property economy.

16 CAPITAL OWNERSHIP FOR CORPORATE EMPLOYEES

SINCE WE TRADITIONALLY THINK of solving our economic problems exclusively through full employment, it is fortunate that the Second Income Plan offers highly industrialized economies like those of the United States and Canada the likelihood of full employment for two to three decades. This can be only an estimate: the actual duration of the full employment phase must depend upon how fast an economy growing at several times its current rate will reach generally affluent levels of production and consumption under highly automated conditions. In less industrialized economies, the Second Income Plan will afford even longer periods of full employment. This is a side effect of building industrial systems large enough to produce general affluence. The full employment called for by this enormous economic growth will be the frantic kind that characterized Germany and Japan during the rebuilding of their industries following World War II.

Every minute of the full employment phase of industrial growth under the Second Income Plan, whether it is twenty or thirty years or longer, will be needed for the gargantuan task of educating a generation of men and women even-

tually to become capable of living in a fully affluent, technologically advanced environment in which there will be
an economic demand for only a small portion of their
potentially available work time. Thirty years is none too
long for educating men and women to live with leisure and
to engage in leisure work. The task will be difficult not only
because so few of our ancestors successfully mastered, or
even had occasion to master, that art; it will be difficult because we are at this very moment perverting almost the
whole of our educational system, formal and informal, into
a training academy for the toil state where neediest redistribution is increasingly disguised as toil. As the need for
legitimate employment has diminished in our purchasing-
power arid economy, the attempts to synthesize it grow
ever more frenzied. In this respect the economy resembles
the uprooted plant which makes a heroic effort to bloom
before it dies.

For several reasons, one of the most important Second
Income Plan techniques for building the second economy
deals with facilitating the acquisition of equity capital by
corporate employees, by means that simultaneously provide
greatly improved sources of financing new capital formation
for the corporate employer.[55]

In the ultimate sense the disabled individual, the in-
firm individual, the noneconomic worker such as the
teacher, the writer, the poet, the playwright, the government employee, the minister, the musician, the actor, the
legislator, the judge, etc., are quite as important consumers
qua consumer as the worker. But the massive physical task
of building the second economy in most countries rests
upon the private enterprise worker; *his* motivation is crucial. Furthermore, since that task will require the fullest
economic employment, leaving us with neither the occasion
nor the inclination to "create" unnecessary jobs as mere

justification for needist distributions, the ultimate goal of
enabling all households (including the households of middle management executives, the most strangely capitalless
class on earth) legitimately to acquire ownership of viable
capital holdings can be achieved largely through techniques
aimed directly at employees.

The basic technique for financing capital ownership
for corporate employees involves the use of employee deferred-compensation plans and trusts that *differ both in
principle and in effectiveness* from such plans and trusts in
general use in the United States today. However, these
plans, which we call Second Income Plan Trusts, or "SIP
Trusts," can qualify, under the proper circumstances, as
stock-bonus plans, profit-sharing plans, or even pension
plans under present provisions of the U.S. Internal Revenue
Code and under the comparable provisions of most state
corporate income tax laws.

The limits of this essay permit only an introduction of
the SIP Trust financing concept. Technical and practical
details cannot be fully discussed here. It should be noted,
however, that a small but representative number of U.S.
corporations, with the advice and assistance of one of the
authors, have already found it a highly effective device for
enabling close-holding owners to sell either the ownership
of the corporation, or a portion of it, to employees who pay
for it out of pre-tax corporate earnings; to provide financing for corporate growth, repayable out of pre-tax corporate
earnings while building capital ownership into employees;
to enable employees of a corporate subsidiary or division,
subject to an antitrust divestiture order or decree, to purchase the subsidiary or division out of pre-tax corporate
earnings, etc.

For the reader not acquainted with the intricacies of the

U.S. Internal Revenue Code and corporate practice with respect to employee deferred-compensation plans that has arisen under it, a brief explanation may be helpful. An employee deferred-compensation plan and trust is a fictitious legal entity established by a trust agreement, usually between the employer corporation and a bank trustee. In legal contemplation, it is an entity separate both from the corporation and from the employees of the corporation. As such, if it "qualifies," i.e., if it meets specified Internal Revenue Code requirements and conforms to applicable regulations issued by the U.S. Treasury Department, *it is exempt from all federal taxation, and also generally all state taxation.* "Contributions" of corporate income to it, within specified limits, are exempt from corporate income taxes, which are 48% at the present federal level (and Congress at this writing is preparing to raise the rate to support mounting warfare and welfare costs), and range from zero to about eight percent at the state level.

Generally speaking, qualified deferred-compensation plans must cover all employees of the corporation, although certain exclusions are permitted. The "accounts" of employees in the trust are made up of allocations of corporate contributions roughly proportionate to the relative compensation each employee currently receives from the corporation. While most plans are designed to distribute the employee's accumulation at retirement, or to his estate in case of death, or upon his separation from the corporation, variations permitting earlier distributions—say of the yield of the employee's account—are possible. Contributions of the corporation into the trust are not taxable to the employee until his interest is withdrawn from the trust, and then at capital-gain rates (maximum 25%) if his entire account is delivered to him within one year. If the distribu-

tions are in the form of the sponsoring corporation's own
stock, the employee, under U.S. tax law, is taxed (at capital-
gain rates) only on the basis of the trust's *cost* of the stock,
and is not taxed on any unrealized appreciation until or
unless he sells the stock. If the employee should die while
any portion of his account in the trust is undistributed and
has named any beneficiary other than his own estate, the
account is free from Federal estate taxation.

While such trusts have been used in a wide number of
variations for years as devices for accumulating additional
compensation for employees out of pre-corporate-tax earnings of the corporation, the SIP Trust and Plan radically
departs from the conventional forms. It differs in concept
and it is enormously more potent, both in providing a
source of financing for the corporation and in enabling the
employees to acquire equity ownership out of future savings, rather than merely out of past savings. This functional
duality has momentous implications for putting the Second
Income Plan into effect. While the discussion and illustra-
tions in this chapter are keyed to U.S. corporate practice and
U.S. tax laws, the basic mechanism of the SIP Trust as a
device for promoting corporate growth while building
capital ownership into employees is of universal application.

Diagram I, which follows, relates to an employee deferred-compensation plan intended to "qualify" as an SIP
Trust under U.S. Internal Revenue Code provisions relating to stock bonus trusts. The diagram should help the
reader understand the mechanics of second income trust
financing.

Note that Diagram I represents only the static relationships
involved in an SIP Trust at a particular moment. Some of
the operational characteristics will be described below. The
features of the SIP Trust which stand out as different from

Diagram I: Second Income Plan Financing

(How to Promote Corporate Growth by Making Your Employees Capital Owners)

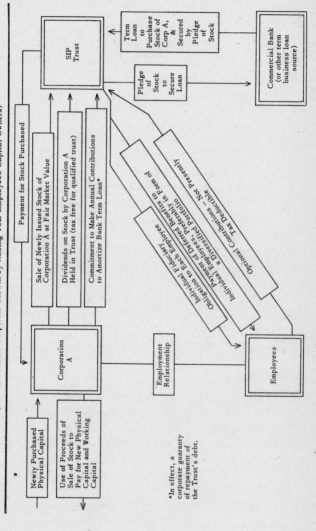

*In effect, a corporate guaranty of repayment of the Trust's debt.

those of conventional profit sharing, pension, and stock bonus plans are:

(1) The funds involved come initially from a credit source, rather than from the internal sources of the corporation. This is the converter device which, in effect, makes corporate credit available to the corporation's employees. It does so in a manner that is more beneficial to the corporation and all its stockholders than if the corporation borrowed directly, since it would then have to repay its obligation out of *after-tax* corporate income.

(2) For credit-worthiness, the lender relies both on the pledge of the securities purchased by the trust with the proceeds of the loan and the general corporate credit in the form of a commitment to make annual contributions sufficient to amortize the debt of the SIP Trust. The trust can also pledge otherwise-free assets to secure such a loan, although preferably it would not do so. Since the obligation is repayable out of untaxed income, and in the United States the combined federal and state corporate tax rate is generally 50% or more, the lender must regard the risk as *twice as safe as if the loan were made directly to the corporation,* since the loan in that case would be repayable in after-tax dollars only.

(3) The trust investments can consist of newly issued corporate stock of the sponsor corporation at a price equal to fair market value. That makes the funds advanced by the lender immediately available for use by the corporation for new capital formation, without dilution or intervention from speculator's profits, as where the corporation's stock has first been sold to the public and is later repurchased by the trust.

(4) The corporation's effective liability, through the guaranty of debt service of the SIP Trust in the form of

annual or other periodic contributions to the trust, is *less* than if the corporation had borrowed directly from the lending source and had invested the proceeds in its expansion. Not only does the stock of the corporation purchased with the loan proceeds stand as a pledge, but in effect, both the principal repayments and interest on the debt are deductible for income tax purposes.

(5) There is no economic dilution of the interest of the existing stockholders of the corporation, since the newly issued stock is sold to the SIP Trust at current fair market value. In fact, precisely the reverse is true: the equity of all stockholders is enriched through the corporation's ability, via the SIP Trust, to *finance new capital formation on pretax corporate income* rather than after-tax corporate income. There is *political dilution* of the present stockholders' equity inasmuch as SIP Trust financing will make stockholders of employees who, some years hence,[56] upon distribution of their holdings to them by the trust, will be able to vote the stock.

Any objections to the economic enfranchisement of the population as a whole must be regarded as unacceptable if (1) the theory of universal capitalism is sound and, (2) it is desirable that all households and individuals be owners of capital equities so that they may be enabled to produce a portion of their incomes through capital ownership. The so-called preemptive rights of stockholders are now rarely recognized in corporate practice; in any case, such preemptive rights are inconsistent with broad capital ownership and hence with a private property economy.

Nor is the objective of equality of economic opportunity contemplated by the Second Income Plan achieved by shunting the investments of newly financed capitalists away from the most profitable and well-established enterprises into new and untried firms. This is the error of Title IV of the "Economic Opportunity Act of 1964"—the U.S. anti-poverty program.

That law enables the Small Business Administration to make loans to struggling small firms or new enterprises in economically depressed areas in order to help them get on their feet. The theory is that this promotes confidence and self-reliance, and enables people to become self-employed. The SBA makes loans of up to twenty-five thousand dollars under this program, and operates training courses on how to run a business. By the end of 1966, after nearly two years of operation, about twenty-five million dollars had been loaned to twenty-five hundred borrowers. Such a program has virtually nothing in common with the Second Income Plan for the following reasons:

A. Any program in the U.S. aimed at building a second economy several times as productive as the present one, and in the course of this task, raising the power of the fifty-nine million families (out of a total of sixty million) who do not own viable capital holdings to buy affluent quantities of goods and services through two sources of income (or through their capital incomes alone when net unemployment arises) must be based upon getting blue-chip stocks into the new capital owner's portfolio. Similarly, it must be based upon producing goods and services by the most efficient enterprises, which are generally large-scale.

B. The Second Income Plan investor must be one who acquires a diversified portfolio of high-grade stocks in the best managed, most seasoned, and most stable businesses. The SBA anti-poverty loans are exactly the opposite. That program reserves the present and future ownership of the prime firms to the minute capital-owning class, and enables a handful of hardy and courageous souls to pit their ill-managed, ill-financed, and generally ill-conceived enterprises against the entrenched giants. With rare exceptions, such a program is nothing but idle lip service to the idea of entrepreneurship; it invites and underwrites almost inevitable disasters.

C. Business in a world starved of consumer purchasing power by virtue of its pre-industrial economic policies, grounded on one-factor economic theories, is fiercely competitive. There is no field of enterprise that does not interest the large, well-established, and well-financed conglomerate corporation of today. From the moment that a small, struggling firm becomes successful, accidentally or otherwise, one or more well-established corporations will seek to take over or destroy its business.

D. There is hardly a line of business in which success is not dependent on automation and economies of scale. In our opinion, the small-business-investment approach is oblivious to these realities.

E. The small-business approach to entrepreneurial training will work best for the small businessman who already has acquired viable holdings of the best corporate equities. He can then fall back on those equities when his small business is overtaken by its virtually certain fate.

(6) Where depreciable property is purchased by the corporation with the proceeds of its sale of stock, the corporation will recover, over the life of the assets, more than 100% of the cost of new capital formation out of taxes, at current U.S. and state corporate income tax rates. At the same time, *it will make capital owners of its employees.* This favorable result is justified from the standpoint of both social and tax policy in a society that recognizes the necessity both of building the second economy and of speedily creating a universal capital-ownership base.

As the stock allocated to employees under the SIP Trust is paid for, dividends on the stock can be passed through the trust to the employees in order to provide them with second incomes. Of course, the SIP Trust can, by virtue of its tax-exempt status, diversify without capital gains tax.[57]

There are as many corporate uses for SIP Trust financing as there are corporate uses for conventional financing, and in most, the superior efficiency of pre-corporate tax dollars over post-tax dollars is just as advantageous as in financing corporate new capital formation. In each instance the building of capital ownership into employees, including management itself, if not the main objective, is a beneficial side effect.

Additional uses include financing of acquisitions; financing sale of subsidiaries or divisions to employees to comply with antitrust divestiture orders or decrees or to simplify corporate structures; financing empire building by entrepreneurs in ways that have the socially desirable side effects of building employee purchasing power, loyalty and motivation; financing diversification of productive operations, etc. Innovative management, labor, and government experts doubtless will discover many others.

17 CAPITAL OWNERSHIP FOR THOSE OUTSIDE THE CORPORATE ENCLAVES

THE FOLLOWING PROPOSALS are based upon the analysis of the inadequacy of conventional corporate finance to bring about universal capitalism, and the proposed alternative method for financing corporate growth through making new capital owners set forth in *The New Capitalists.*[58] There, Kelso and Adler violated a taboo imposed by the conventional wisdom. They asked—and answered—the question: "What is the function of *present capital ownership* in the process of financing *newly formed capital,* under conventional financing techniques?" The answer, they concluded, is that existing financial or tangible capital is put at risk to *insure* against the possibility that newly formed capital either *may not* pay for itself within a reasonable time, or that if it does so, the wealth it produces *may not be used* to make that reimbursement. The practice of using existing capital for this insurance purpose is part of the conventional invisible structure of the economy; it is the basis for vesting in existing capital owners the ownership of virtually all newly formed capital.

Kelso and Adler concluded that the insuring function could be better accomplished through methods long used in the insuring of financial risks, and in particular by means similar to the Federal Housing Insurance Plan in the United States. Their proposal is designed to *break* the historical connection between the ownership of existing capital and the right of present capital owners to acquire ownership of *all* newly formed capital. That aspect of conventional finance (said the authors) is responsible for creating a narrow and stationary ownership base. The goal of universal capitalism is, of course, the exact opposite. Our proposals, in brief, are these:

(1) We would create a commercial counterpart of the FHA Insurance Agency, which might be called the Capital Diffusion Insurance Corporation (CDIC). In the event that private insurers should not wish to provide this type of insurance through a privately organized syndicate, it could be done by a self-liquidating government insurance agency like the FHA. Such a vast new field of underwriting, once opened, may well require both public and private exploitation.

(2) The function of the insurance corporation, or the insurance corporations, would be to insure lenders that make financed capitalist loans (for the dual purpose of creating new capital-owning families and financing new capital formation) against failure of the new plant and equipment, structures, farms, etc., represented by the stocks in the financed portfolios to pay off their purchase costs within a prescribed financing period. The projects being financed would have to pass the same feasibility tests that the financial world employs today.

(3) The CDIC financing program ultimately is intended, together with SIP Trusts for employees, to en-

tirely replace internal corporate financing, but it is not intended to displace—*only to complement*—other conventional business finance.

(4) Should the accumulated financial savings (time deposits, savings and loan deposits, insurance company and mutual fund assets, etc.) available in the economy at any time be inadequate to meet the demands for loan funds for SIP Trust financing and CDIC financing, we propose that CDIC loan paper and SIP Trust loans held by commercial banks should be made discountable through the federal reserve system. Such a necessity could well arise in a developing economy or in any economy where the growth rate rapidly accelerates under the symmetrical expansion of corporate productive capacity and consumer purchasing power. A monetary system which in effect *monetizes new capital formation* under controlled conditions where top corporate and financial executive feasibility scrutiny is a prerequisite to the new capital formation coming into existence in each corporation, *would be the first logical and totally flexible monetary system in history*. It would monetize that factor of production which determines primarily the growth of business, and which, in an industrial or industrializing economy, primarily is responsible for producing the goods and services that money is used to buy. Under such a monetary system, new money introduced into the economy in the form of payments to individuals engaged in building new plants and equipment is always directly coupled with increases in the power of the economy to produce and to consume useful goods and services.

Compare this proposal, for example, with Keynesian economic techniques under which deficit government financing is used to pay for a variety of activities which have no connection with producing useful goods and services, such as the space program, production of overkill hardware,

leaf raking, and the like. Or compare it with the needist
expedient of paying workers more for producing no more,
or more often, for producing less, or for producing nothing.
All of these "new economics" techniques are actually the
inherently inflationary expedients of pre-industrial, one-
factor Keynesian economics. Either the additional purchasing power generated must be offset by taxation, or by inflation. Such is not the case with monetary expansion
through the monetization of new capital formation under
the Second Income Plan.

It is unlikely that the discounting of financed capitalist
loan paper would need to be utilized in the United States
in the early stages of the Second Income Plan, although the
lack of flexibility in the money supply of the United States
under present arrangements leaves that question in some
doubt. However, in numerous economies around the world
—Canada, for example—the lack of financing flexibility
in the domestic monetary system is encouraging U.S. corporations, swollen with earnings withheld from stockholders, to acquire their productive capital. Such economies,
concerned with the question of "economic nationalism,"
may well find the discount technique immediately beneficial. In the developing economies, the discounting of financed capitalist loans through a central bank, perhaps
aided by guaranties from advanced foreign economies desiring to sell them capital goods and technical services, appears to us to be indispensable to the achievement of their
economic goals.[58a]

Keynesian economists, properly sensitive to the inflationary impact of economic proposals, since their own techniques have proved to be as inflationary in practice as they
are in theory, are the first to exclaim that the monetizing
of new capital formation would be inflationary. They are
mistaken. Newly formed capital in well-managed businesses

(and the Second Income Plan should be employed only to accelerate growth and broaden ownership in well-managed businesses) pays for itself in a reasonably short period, rarely more than five years. Thereafter the new productive capital, under depreciation and amortization accounting practices in general use today, continues to produce net income indefinitely. It thus adds vastly more to the supply of goods and services than it adds in the form of new money representing the cost of newly formed capital. Consequently, the steady and relentless effect of Second Income Plan financing techniques is *deflationary,* i.e., to slowly raise the purchasing power of the consumer's income, but without tending to deprive him of a source of income. Because hardening money has traditionally been accompanied by income loss from unemployment, as must be the case under one-factor economic concepts, we have forgotten that one of the benefits of technological advance, in a rational economy, would be the rising purchasing power of money.

While the subject needs careful study because of its many ramifications, it would seem that a good case could be made for a low-administered interest rate on both SIP trust loans and CDIC insured loans. This is particularly true when the economy reaches the point of monetizing new capital formation discussed above. Then the process of financing economic expansion is running on *pure credit,* and the argument that bank depositors' "savings" are being loaned does not hold. Nevertheless, because interest rates do have reverberations throughout the economy, all aspects of this question must be thoroughly analyzed.

Nevertheless, it will be necessary to avoid any possible preliminary inflationary impact as the result of phasing the Second Income Plan into an economy already suffering from the inflationary effects of a large and imaginative variety of needist expedients. It should be readily feasible

to reduce governmental expenditures for the numerous
needist make-work programs already mentioned, and needist redistributive welfare programs; the reductions could
be carefully correlated to balance the credit used to expand
productive enterprises providing *useful* employment producing *useful* goods and services.

(5) The source of stock to be purchased by financed new
capital owners would be capital stock *newly issued* by well-
established corporations expanding to build the second
economy. In the United States, the current rate of expansion of about sixty billion dollars per year, if financed entirely in this manner, would be enough to allocate about
four thousand dollars of stock per year for purchase by each
of fifteen million low-income families. We would expect the
growth rate of the United States economy, under the Second
Income Plan, to treble within the first five years *without inflation*.

(6) The head of a low-income family would go to his
commercial bank or other qualified lender. After establishing his eligibility, he could borrow, for example, four thousand dollars each year for five years on CDIC-insured loans
which would be without risk to the bank or to the borrower.
He would make a small down payment of perhaps two
hundred dollars. An escrow account would be established
in the bank and after consulting with the borrower, the
trust officer would purchase for the borrower's account a
diversified portfolio of previously qualified, newly issued
corporate equities. These would be retained in the bank
escrow until the portfolio is paid for out of its earnings. At
the end of five years, the cost value of the portfolio would
be, therefore, twenty thousand dollars. (As the second economy grows, these loan limits might be increased, both to
adequately finance accelerating economic growth and to
increase the productive power, and thus the buying power,
of the consumers.)

(7) Corporations qualifying for CDIC financing would be contractually committed to pay out annually a high percentage of their earnings, and would be assured of the availability of future financing through the CDIC plan so long as feasibility tests are met. Corporate income tax laws would be amended to make dividends payable into CDIC financing escrows deductible by the corporation; thus, one step would be taken toward repeal of the corporate income tax. Personal income-tax laws would be amended to make dividends nontaxable to the buyer until his stock is paid for, after which it would be fully taxable.

(8) Dividends at the rate of the average pre-tax earnings of the top two thousand United States corporations (20% to 30% on invested capital) would pay off each loan, principal and interest, in five to seven years. In many developing economies, the rate of earnings on invested capital averages much higher.

(9) The financed family would then own a twenty thousand dollar portfolio of diversified top-grade securities, capable on the average of yielding in the United States economy an income of about eighty dollars per week, or about four thousand dollars per year under current conditions. If it is desirable to accelerate the receipt of second incomes by families and individuals buying capital estates, less than the total yield of the stocks in the escrow account might be applied to repayment of the financing loan, with the balance being paid out currently to the stock purchaser. For example, 100% of the portfolio income might be applied to loan repayment until 25% of the loan has been paid off. From that time until the loan principal balance has been reduced to 50% of the original, the portfolio income might be applied 75% to principal and interest of the loan and 25% paid currently to the financed capital purchaser. A similar step-adjustment might be made when the loan is 50% paid off, and when it is 75% paid off. While this ar-

rangement would extend the loan repayment period, it might be justified, under some circumstances, in order to accelerate economic growth.

The following Diagrams II and III will help to illustrate the plan.

Only the rudiments of the proposals can be presented in a general survey of a subject which is necessarily technical. But these basic techniques for building the industrial productive power of the second economy, and simultaneously the power of millions of families to participate in production through their ownership of capital as well as through their employment (to the extent that an honest demand for such employment exists) offer almost unlimited possibilities for variation.

Nor will we here digress from our basic purpose, which is the introduction of the Second Income Plan, to discuss (1) the great utility of the Second Income Plan for returning most economic planning from the government level to the business management and labor union level, while strengthening government's ability to make effective its national economic policy; (2) the new and infinitely more potent antitrust weapons provided to government through the financing and monetary mechanisms of the Second Income Plan; these can expedite the growth of competition where it is needed, while making more capital-owning families in the process.

Whether men can adjust themselves by the time the second economy has been brought into existence (perhaps twenty-five years after the task is begun) to an economy in which their personal efforts and energies would be largely directed to the unlimited work of leisure—to education, the arts, science, sports, religion, philosophy, statesmanship, and the like, remains to be seen.[59] We are confident, however, of this: such a life is in accord with the tendencies of man's nature. Human beings are far more likely to adapt to it than to the consequences of any of the needist alternatives which, at best, can only compel all men to share poverty and the status of wards of charity in a totalitarian toil state.

Diagram II: How the Second Income Plan
Finances the Purchase of Stock by Individual Families

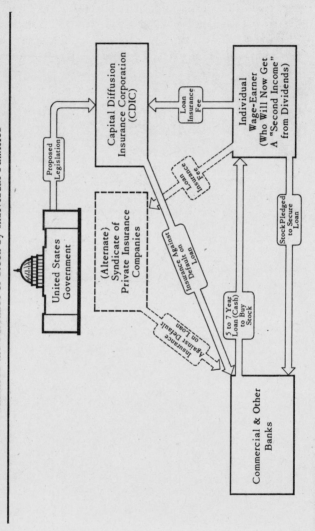

Diagram III: How stocks pay for themselves under the Second Income Plan

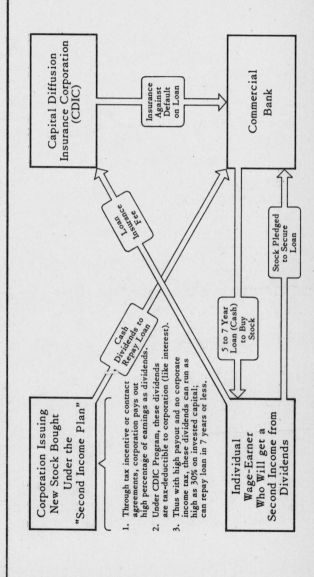

Capital Diffusion Insurance Corporation (CDIC)

Insurance Against Default on Loan

Commercial Bank

Loan Insurance Fee

Cash Dividends to Repay Loan

5 to 7 Year Loan (Cash) to Buy Stock

Stock Pledged to Secure Loan

Corporation Issuing New Stock Bought Under the "Second Income Plan"

1. Through tax incentive or contract agreements, corporation pays out high percentage of earnings as dividends.

2. Under CDIC Program, these dividends are tax-deductible to corporation (like interest).

3. Thus with high payout and no corporate income tax, these dividends can run as high as 30% on invested capital; can repay loan in 7 years or less.

Individual Wage-Earner Who Will get a Second Income from Dividends

PART III

Economic Planning and the Theory of Universal Capitalism

18 PLANNING BEGINS

WITH A GOAL

MANY POLITICAL GROUPS in the United States today take a dim view of economic planning. Part of its sinister image is a legacy from classical economics. The very idea of economic planning conflicts with the mystical dogma that the "unseen hand" of the free market is superior to any rational plan requiring legislative, administrative or institutional action. Nor has the unwholesome aura been dispelled by the fact that in the Soviet Union, Great Britain and the continental countries, economic planning has been synonymous with plotting the redistribution of wealth and purchasing power in accordance with need, as determined by the ruling bureaucracy.

It is hardly surprising, then, that we often find the owners of productive capital and those beholden to them opposing economic planning for some of the same reasons that politicians, deriving their support from the nonaffluent, favor it. On the one hand, economic planning has traditionally threatened the right of capital owners endlessly to accumulate and concentrate the ownership of the nonhuman factor of production; on the other, it has been the instrument used by the capitalless masses to return wealth and income to those they erroneously believe to be its producers—the workers, or those who can make no other legitimate claim upon income except through their unsaleable labor.

Advocates of economic planning are quick to remind the opposition that the first ones to decry the use of planning at the national level are those same individuals who most meticulously employ it in the management of their businesses and personal affairs. The point is unassailable. No businessman today would think of operating even a small enterprise without a plan. For all except those who believe in the "unseen hand" theory, a planless economy is an irrational one. Certainly the theory of universal capitalism implies a plan. If the proper goal of an industrial (or industrializing) economy is the production and distribution of general affluence, and if each consumer unit (household or single individual) must, from the nature of things, itself produce the affluence it wishes to consume, the importance of economic planning within the framework of the theory is evident.

Economic planning as the world has experienced it so far has been based upon the pre-industrial notion that labor is the only factor of production; that the foremost goal of the economy is to keep labor fully employed, and that all consumers can be adequately supplied with purchasing power by the coercive or legislative adjustment of wage levels, or by other needist methods of redistributing income. Planners tend to look upon men as "resources" to be kept busy. But wealth is really produced by capital, as well as by labor, and it is capital that is responsible for a progressively greater part of the productive input. Furthermore, men are not resources. They are the lords of the earth, intended not to toil for subsistence but to master nature and to make her work for them. They reach their highest stature in an environment of affluent leisure. It is hardly surprising, therefore, that one-factor economic planning has disastrous consequences in the reality of a two-factor world.

One of the first casualties of toil-oriented economic planning is leisure. Sebastian de Grazia has documented the truth that our widely acclaimed increase in "leisure" is a myth.[60] Nor is leisure, as Josef Pieper reminds us, merely "free time" or time off from work. A society without leisure, which has commercialized the essentially noneconomic work of civilization, such as the arts, science, literature, medicine, law, teaching, nursing, etc., discourages creativity. While society's most creative members pay the immediate cost in the form of boredom, frustration and sterility, the resulting cultural and spiritual impoverishment diminishes everyone. The hatreds and frictions generated by redistribution must also be charged to toil-fixated planning. As for the failure to achieve general affluence, no toil-oriented economy has ever dared to claim it as a goal.

Economic planning in the form of needist redistribution, in short, leads sooner or later to the totalitarian toil state. It is true that the road may lead through fields of apparent economic progress, where the erosion of property in the nonhuman factor of production is disguised as rising personal, business and government debt. But the pleasant vista is sheer façade. On state visits of Catherine the Great to the lands she had given him, Count Potëmkin is alleged to have masked the wretched peasant hovels along the Tsarina's carriage route behind painted stage flats. Rolling past idyllic cottage scenery and smiling serfs, Catherine was deceived into believing that communities Potëmkin was secretly ruining were paragons of contentment and affluence. Redistributive economic planning makes a similar use of debt.

Clearly it is not planning as such, but planning built

upon deficient concepts and around a false goal that has yielded such grotesque results. Planning which harnesses the motivational power of the proprietary instinct will have quite different effects from planning intended to frustrate it. Planning that extends the private ownership of productive property to all and that harnesses the power of property to build an orderly and stable society will have an outcome quite different from planning designed both to concentrate the ownership and to destroy the integrity of private property. Planning which is based upon recognition of capital as a co-factor of production, which enables every citizen to acquire reasonable amounts of capital in the name of equal economic opportunity, and which at the same time discourages the institutions that endlessly concentrate the ownership of the most productive factor, will enhance the lives and liberties of individuals, instead of constricting them.

Within the concept of the theory of universal capitalism and the Second Income Plan, economic planning will involve the rational design of the invisible structure of enterprise and of the invisible sector of the economy. But there is another dimension to economic planning—it is *timing*. Wise timing depends upon understanding the difference between the urgent and the important. This is the subject of the next chapter.

19 THE LAW OF URGENT

AND IMPORTANT

HUMAN AFFAIRS are governed by a dual hierarchy of values, each corresponding to one of the two sides of man's nature. The priority order of particular activities on these tables of values is inverse, so that an activity which occupies first place on one is in last place on the other.

Man is an animal, and his animal needs and wants are the subject matter of economics. But he is also a spiritual being, with a mind unique in the natural order; he is a civilized, or *human* being. It is from the dual nature of man as both animal and human that the dual scale of values governing his life arises. One is a hierarchy of urgency; the other is a hierarchy of importance. The history of man, at least as we read it, leaves no doubt that he places the highest value on the goods of the mind and of the spirit—what Plato called "the wares of the soul"; that in the human scale of things, it is the goods of civilization—the arts, the sciences, religion, education, philosophy, statesmanship and the like, that weigh heaviest. Despite much particular evidence to the contrary, man's civilization as a whole testifies to that truth.

It is equally clear, however, that for all but the most

exceptional human beings, the goods and services that minister to the need and desire for creature comforts weigh heaviest on the scale of urgency. True, not all economic goods and services are of equal urgency; they will be assigned different urgency-priorities by different individuals, although the patterns of precedence are remarkably consistent. Nor are the goods of civilization assigned the same importance-priority by different individuals, for here individuality itself is paramount. But for men as a whole, the general rule is that the goods of civilization are more important, while the physical goods and services of economics are more urgent. It is only when man's material needs and desires are satisfied and he is secure in his belief that they will continue to be satisfied—when, in a word, he becomes affluent—that the urgency of economic matters disappears, and the truly important things move into the foreground of consciousness. In the presence of poverty, all human affairs are dominated by the urgency of things economic; the importance of the goods of civilization is obscured, and even repudiated.

Economic planning for a free industrial society that fails to take into account the significance of the inverse dual scale of values implicit in man's nature is predestined to error. The lesson to be learned from man's inverse dual scale of values, for all practical purposes, is simple: solve the economic problem of society first, and a flood tide of the goods of civilization will follow. We believe this development to be not only possible, but inevitable. For when general affluence is achieved within a society, man's relentless urge for creative conquest, except in the case of senseless and incorrigible greed, has no outlet other than through the works of civilization.

Much of the confusion, insecurity, misery and danger of the world today grows directly out of the failure of the industrialized nations, particularly the United States, to recognize the difference between the urgent and the important, and to give priority to the urgent.

Take, for example, the space race. The conquest of space is unquestionably important. Its technological value is incalculable; its educational value and its appeal to man's imagination is immense. It appeals to the mind and spirit, whose goods and values make up the hierarchy of the important that is the work of civilization. But by no objective standard, we submit, can the conquest of space be appraised as *urgent* under present circumstances in the world.

We live in a world where the standard of living of the unindustrialized nations is falling, at the same time that the citizens of those nations are discovering that without the fruits of industrialization, life is intolerable. Our impoverished world desperately needs the technical competence and skills that we are diverting into the conquest of space. That which is important, we are doing, and doing brilliantly. That which is urgent and which, if left to run its own violent course, will destroy the world and civilization, we do not at all, or we do haphazardly and badly. By violating the law of urgent and important, an inherently important scientific undertaking is transformed into a disaster. The magnitude of that disaster can only be appreciated by the historians of the future.

Nor do we think that the space race can be considered urgent from a military standpoint, particularly in view of the extent to which we are otherwise producing military overkill power. In a remarkable pronouncement to the American Society of Newspaper Editors at its May, 1966 meeting in Montreal, Canada, Secretary of Defense Robert S. McNamara said:

> We still tend to conceive of national security almost solely as a state of armed readiness: a vast, awesome arsenal of weaponry . . . A nation can reach the point at which it does

not buy more security for itself simply by buying more military hardware—we are at that point.[61]

Our failure to provide sound and intelligent leadership for the developing economies in the urgent areas of economic development concepts and industrialization must contribute to the rise of hostile political movements within, and alliances between, the impoverished nations of the world. Both reactions will greatly increase our military risk, whereas a policy of according priority to assisting the developing economies both to industrialize and to raise the economic productiveness of all their citizens would diminish and, in many cases, eliminate it.

Let us take another example of the contemporary tendency to confuse the urgent and the important. Idealism is one of the most precious characteristics of youth. Perhaps the best test of whether or not a society is self-renewing in the sense John Gardner has used the term[62] is the degree to which the idealism of the young survives its early encounters with the institutional realities. If young people are disillusioned by those encounters, if their idealism is tarnished, if—worst of all—they find that they have been misled by their elders, the society is in deep trouble.

When the United States calls upon its young people, at an age when most of them would otherwise be entering the labor market, to follow their ideals and to go out into the world to "do good"; to assist the people of the developing economies in the fields of education, agriculture, sanitation, organization of industry, and in many other areas, it is calling upon them to do work of great importance. It is also distracting them from things that are, to the youths themselves, urgent, whether or not they themselves realize it.

Once young people have finished their educations, the next order of business is the attainment of some degree of affluence. Much of the quality of their future life, as well as their later attitude toward society, will depend on their success in solving their personal economic problems. Their chances of winning the mate they want, of establishing a secure material base for family life, of enriching their experience, of ensuring freedom of action and choice, of cultivating their taste, of acquiring standing in the community—all of these things we ask youth to postpone or to jeopardize in order to follow the idealistic calling of helping the less fortunate. While the young may endure poverty more blithely than their elders, as normal human beings they are still subject to the law of urgent and important. Some years downstream, many of these young idealists are going to discover that in serving the latter and neglecting the former, they have aggravated their own economic problems. They are also going to discover that most of what they have struggled so idealistically to accomplish will have been destroyed or made ineffective by the foreign, military and business policies pursued by the very government that spurred them on to self-sacrifice in the name of humanity, brotherhood and peace. Nor will the realization that by organizing and directing youthful idealism government was able to temporarily remove from the labor market tens of thousands of young people otherwise difficult or impossible to employ under our pre-industrial economic concepts make the awakening of the young any less cataclysmic.

If the work of the Peace Corps is important for its own sake, and not just as a means of diverting young people from discovering that their elders do not know very much about economics or running societies in general, the law of the urgent and important would suggest a different procedure. Within the top ten percent of wealth-holding families in the United States—or even better, within the top five percent—are many highly competent and experienced men and women who have provided, often many times over, for their urgent economic needs and wants. These men and women have accumulated capital holdings which assure them (or would assure them, were we to stop eroding away the property base in capital) of general affluence for the rest of their lives. The tutelary function of good government should encourage those who have provided for their urgent economic needs and wants to change the focus of their energies to what is important, just as surely as it should provide true equality of economic opportunity for those whose economic needs and wants are critically urgent. We do not here criticize the generous idealism of the young, but only the wisdom of a government policy that is, as applied to them, oblivious to the law of urgent and important.

The Keynesian economists habitually disregard the law of urgent and important. At all times and in impressive numbers, they are to be found demanding that governments incur great debt in order to build all manner of *nonurgent* public works *as a means of providing employment for the unemployed.* Of course, some public works are urgent. Adequate roads over which commerce may pass; bridges that shorten transport distances and reduce waste of time and resources; harbors that facilitate ocean commerce—such things are infrastructure improvements that are economically urgent. In contrast to these, however, are dozens of varieties of amenity-type public improvements. Unquestionably they are important; but they are not urgent. Normal market forces and the democratic procedures for approving taxes and bond issues to erect them would relegate them to a later time, after urgent economic needs have been satisfied.

Nevertheless, proponents of Keynesian economics would override market and democratic legal procedures for evaluating the urgency of public amenities. Such projects help synthesize the toil required to keep the economy running under preindustrial one-factor economic concepts. That consideration, in the Keynesian view, outweighs the democratic niceties. To the extent that the electorate is circumvented and amenity-type public works commissioned through legislative and administrative action, the energies and resources of those involved are absorbed by the important, although nonurgent. But the urgent task of building a second economy, and financing it in such a manner as to enable labor-dependent families and individuals to own the *other* factor of production in amounts large enough to serve as significant income sources is neglected. Because the important is confused with the urgent, and the law governing the priority of the two is disregarded, we are afflicted with social misplanning on a gargantuan scale.

Another painful example of disregarding the law of urgent and important is provided by the civil rights movement in the United States. There is no question that it is of the greatest importance for members of racial minorities, particularly the large Negro minority, to establish a status of social and cultural equality with members of the white majority. But what the individual members of those minorities need—even more critically than the population of the United States as a whole—is *affluence*. Problems of social and cultural equality, although important, cannot be solved until the urgent economic problem is successfully disposed of. Only now are some of the minority-group leaders beginning to realize the priority of the urgent, and how much of the present so-called "race problem" has grown directly from its neglect. In a statement issued November 3, 1966, at the Statue of Liberty, the National Committee of Negro Churchmen declared:

. . . The slaves were freed in 1863, but the nation refused to give them land to make that emancipation meaningful. Simultaneously, the nation was giving away millions of acres in the Midwest and West—a gift marked 'for whites only.' Thus, an economic floor was placed under the new peasants from Europe, but America's oldest peasantry was provided only an abstract freedom. In the words of Frederick Douglass, emancipation made the slaves 'free to hunger; free to the winter and rains of heaven . . . free without roofs to cover them or bread to eat or land to cultivate . . . We gave them freedom and famine at the same time. The marvel is that they still live.'[63]

In the belief that man's most critical problem in the modern world is economic, and that unless he solves the urgent he will never have the chance to confront the inherently important, let us see how economic planning might help achieve the goals of the theory of universal capitalism through the Second Income Plan.

20 ECONOMIC PLANNING AT THE GOVERNMENT LEVEL

THE ECONOMIC-PLANNING FUNCTIONS of government, both at the state or provincial level and at the federal level, necessary to support and implement the theory of universal capitalism and the Second Income Plan are for the most part implicit in the theory. In the Appendix will be found a suggested text for policy legislation adopting universal capitalist goals into the economy of the United States. The guiding considerations of a universal capitalist strategy may be summarized as follows:

(1) Since new capital formation is the chief source of increased output of goods and services, the rate of new capital formation must be accelerated until it approaches, as nearly as possible, the controlling physical limits of the economy. The immediate goal is the building of a Second Economy large enough to produce general affluence.

(2) The invisible structures behind each step of new capital formation must be designed to contribute to the building of viable holdings of capital ownership in consumer units that do not already own such holdings. Here the goal is the harnessing of full aggregate consumer de-

mand. All households must be enabled to engage in production both through their employment, to the extent that the prevailing state of technology calls for it, and through their capital ownership. The economic power of the economy to consume goods and services must be raised by raising the power of each consumer unit to produce goods and services. Physical needs and wants must be matched with productive power sufficient to satisfy them.

(3) The credit system of the economy should be used primarily to finance new capital formation and the building of new viable capital estates. Only secondarily should it be used to finance consumer goods. Its objective should be to raise productive power so that consumption can be financed as fully as possible out of current earnings rather than out of borrowings. Of course expensive consumer items such as houses and perhaps automobiles may continue to require consumer finance, but, with rising incomes and diminishing prices, it should be easy drastically to shorten credit terms in order to minimize loss of purchasing power through interest.

(4) Private property must be protected by the legal system, with particular emphasis on dynamic private property in the nonhuman factor of production. "If you own it, you are entitled to what it produces"—that axiom provides one of the strongest blocks for building the invisible structure of the universal capitalist economy. Property is the conduit that connects the nonhuman factor of production with individuals. It is the keystone of the arch of economic justice. Equally basic is the protection of each individual's private property right in his own labor power.

(5) A new antimonopoly concept needs to be introduced into national economic planning. Its objective would be the avoidance of undue concentration of the power to produce wealth in any individual. The production of wealth is a means to an end, consumption. Aggregate pro-

duction and aggregate consumption are two halves of a natural equation. If some individuals accumulate the power to produce *more* than they can consume, or intend to consume within a reasonable time, it is inevitable that others will be forced to produce less than they desire to consume.

That imbalance gives rise to the entire catalogue of economic ills that beset societies structured on pre-industrial concepts. Of course, perfect precision in the matching of productive power and affluent consumption is neither possible nor necessary. But soundly planned monetary policies can easily eliminate the ancient tendency of traditional financing techniques to fulfill the Biblical prophecy of "unto every one that hath shall be given." It is economically unsound, socially unjust and practically unworkable for those households and individuals who already own most of the economy's existing assets to be automatically given ownership of all the newly formed capital. Applied to individuals, the anticoncentration principle is a necessary and long-overdue supplement to traditional antitrust policy as practiced in the United States to maintain market competition.

(6) The planned optimum withdrawal of government from all but absolutely irreducible welfare functions should take place as second incomes flow to more and more consumer units. As the power to produce wealth is extended to all households and individuals in the economy, it will be less and less necessary to distribute wealth on the basis of need. To be sure, some private charity and public welfare may be required even in an economy that has virtually achieved general affluence. But the objective of economic planning in a universal capitalist economy is to reduce both the need for public welfare and private charity to an absolute minimum. Every individual's human dignity requires that he enjoy general affluence, and that *he produce it*.

(7) Planning by government should focus on building

and diffusing the private ownership of economic productive power. Under the techniques of the Second Income Plan, there is no reason to finance any productive enterprise in such a manner that it becomes owned by government. No matter how vast the enterprise, providing only that it is economically feasible, its newly formed capital will pay the cost of formation within a reasonable period of years. Through the magic of the corporation, its invisible structure can be so designed that its equity shares can be owned by any number of individuals. When the new or expanded enterprise has paid for itself (that is, when it has paid its cost of capital formation and interest carrying charges), it can then function to produce income for its owners.

The separation of economic power, represented increasingly by the ownership of productive capital, and political power is the very heart of a free society. Government ownership of productive capital is invariably a step in the direction of totalitarian concentration of power.

(8) Just as government planning under pre-industrial economic concepts paves the way for the totalitarian toil state by making perpetual full employment necessary regardless of the technical requirements of industry, agriculture and trade, so government planning under universal capitalist concepts will prepare the way for the leisure society.

As the urgent demands for general affluence are met, the important work of civilization moves into its place. The production and distribution of useful goods and services fade into the background. Of course the generally affluent society will require a ceaseless flow of goods and services. But with the burden of production placed largely on the nonhuman factor, and with the ownership of that factor diffused throughout the society so that each consumer unit may produce affluence for itself, economic affairs will occupy but a fraction of the population's productive and creative energies. Full employment should continue to be the social ideal of the generally affluent society, but the definition of "full employment" should change with advancing technology so that it comes increasingly to mean leisure work, and decreasingly subsistence work.

(9) Government planning can successfully conserve natural resources when the imperative of economic full employment no longer dominates the society. Then it will no longer be necessary to squander resources in the attempt to legitimate income distribution through make-work.

(10) One of government's planning efforts under a universal capitalist regime would be devoted to diffusing economic risks throughout large portions of the population. Some of the most obvious steps in that direction would be in the form of credit regulations calculated to assure the diversification of financed capitalist portfolios; planning the balanced acquisition in financed capitalist portfolios of long-term and short-term investments, and the like.

(11) Planning should include steps to reduce government make-work employment and employment in needist redistribution as the productive power of households generally is raised through acquisition of the other factor of production.

(12) An important goal of government planning in a universal capitalist economy would be the eventual elimination of government debt. Perpetual government debt is a direct measure of the inadequacy of underlying economic concepts to deal with the real world. In that debt is lumped all the needist redistribution, the concentrated ownership of financial capital by the few, the price of governmental make-work disguised as military overkill production, space waste, subsidization of various kinds of income-legitimating activity not supported by market demand, etc.

A generally affluent society employing universal capitalist concepts would have no debt other than that which might arise from minimal and temporary budget errors or unanticipated emergencies. The deficit financing called for by pre-industrial Keynesian economic concepts would give way to debt-free government.

(13) Planning should encourage corporations and individuals to pattern their international development activity on the theory of universal capitalism. This would open up world markets for sophisticated capital goods, technological and professional know-how, construction skills and scientific talent. It would at the same time vastly speed up the industrialization of the underdeveloped parts of the world. Moreover, the industrial systems thus built would be orderly and self-sustaining, as Second Income Plan techniques are used to simultaneously raise productive power and the power of the citizens of the host countries to engage in production both through their labor and their growing capital ownership. Such techniques also would make possible and actively encourage the growth of free, democratic societies with large, stable, middle classes.[64]

For corporations engaging or desiring to engage in an international business, the planning objectives indicated by the theory of universal capitalism are parallel to those applicable within the corporation's home economy. The income derived by its constituents in the host economy—i.e., those who engage in production through it, either as employees, or as stockholders, or as both—should be commensurate with the value of the goods and services it adds to the host economy. It should, in short, after recovering its capital costs and a reasonable return, annually add as much purchasing power to those areas of the economy that form the market for its goods and services as will enable them to purchase the equivalent of its annual sales in that economy. This enlightened corporate strategy would have the effect of gradually internationalizing the great corporations and their constituencies, spreading not only their powerful production facilities, but their ownership with its economic benefits around the world. Such a commercial and economic prelude to the concept of one world would have only salutary long-run political implications.

The end result would be the opposite of "economic imperialism," a term often used by the poor nations to express their resentment of the ownership by foreigners of the productive capital within their borders. It is a shrewd and proper resentment. For the most part, the poor nations welcome and earnestly plead for the productive and managerial know-how of the industrial nations. What they deplore is the ownership of their newly acquired industrial capital by foreign corporations in which their own citizens do not have equivalent broadly diffused equity interests.

21 ENVIRONMENTAL PLANNING UNDER UNIVERSAL CAPITALISM

ENVIRONMENTAL PLANNING—the planning of the residential and work environment of individuals, of central cities and suburbs, of new cities, of recreational areas, other public amenities and industrial parks—long ago outdistanced the economic concepts with which it today must cope. Although the scientific, engineering and managerial disciplines promise to provide an affluent stream of goods and services (produced largely by machines), one-factor economic concepts operate continually to defeat that promise. Because men who are not connected by dependable property rights to the productive power of the nonhuman factor of production are economically helpless, the effects of these concepts are woven into the political fabric of every country. The purchasing-power shortages, synthesized toil and general economic frustration to which single-factor thinking gives rise unfailingly defeat man's efforts to create the comfortable and pleasing human environment that is technologically achievable.

The environmental planner, whether he is a public

official, private development entrepreneur, contractor, architect or other consultant, or simply the individual planning his own home and garden, his recreation, and his travel, will enter a new world in a universal capitalist economy.

It becomes easier to separate production activity from living space as increasing numbers of individuals produce progressively more of their income vicariously through their ownership of capital. It becomes easier to build new towns and cities when increased new capital formation and the opportunities of the residents to engage in production both through their employment and through their capital ownership grow in concert. The means provided by the Second Income Plan for financing whatever amount of new capital formation may be required to meet consumer market demand (subject only to the physical limitations discussed earlier)[65] will remove the chief impediment to building the estimated five hundred new cities the United States will need by the year 2000.

In every economy in which Keynesian concepts are employed today, the labor costs of land development, construction, and the manufacturing of consumer hard goods (like all other labor costs) are increasingly bloated with welfare, while the effective physical productive input of the labor involved diminishes. All of us are much too familiar with the result. Less and less land per dwelling is used, and less and less space is included in each residential unit. Ornamentation, spaciousness, tasteful design and arrangement, richness of texture, and most other forms of environmental beauty have vanished from all but the most opulent establishments. The quality, beauty, and durability of furnishings have steadily diminished. Spiraling inflationary welfare costs have so bloated the cost of construction that many great enterprises, such as rapid transit systems, air terminals, new cities, and similar projects, are impossible to build as sound planning initially conceived them.

Laboristic redistribution has outrun the means of financing large-scale projects. The acceleration of cost increases in major projects is, in many instances, outpacing the ability of the machinery of public finance to raise new funds during the course of construction. Only the recognition that there are two factors of production, and the enabling of progressively more of the population to engage in economic production through both of them, can reverse this degenerative economic spiral.

As economies come under the influence of the Second Income Plan, and the niggardly rationing of labor as a means of legitimating more worker incomes is eliminated, we can anticipate a revival of craftsmanship in every area of economic activity. Men can then afford to engage in productive activities in which they can take pride, for their employment will no longer be the battleground of power blocs trying to redistribute wealth and income coercively. Leisure and the vicarious production of wealth through ownership of the nonhuman factor of production go together. As leisure increases, so will the opportunities for the environmental planners and those who execute their concepts.

As to the planning of public amenities, experience testifies to the fact that affluent neighborhoods and areas have always had them. They are the mark of affluent communities. Nothing is more inconsistent with the evidence than J.K. Galbraith's complaint that affluent societies neglect the "public sector." The truth is that the affluent resent, and will always resent, paying not only for their share of public amenities, but the share of the vastly greater numbers of nonaffluent. In other words, they resent and will oppose the use of public works as a means of redistributing the wealth produced primarily by their capital.

One thing about the future is certain: public improvements will reach the epitome of beauty and grandeur only in the generally affluent society.

22 BUSINESS PLANNING
UNDER UNIVERSAL CAPITALISM

FOR REASONS ALREADY DISCUSSED, we conclude that the invisible structure of modern business enterprise is defective. Guided by one-factor economic philosophies which are oblivious to the function of private property and which focus public and private attention only upon employment as a means of connecting men with the income-producing power of the production process, private enterprise has progressed to its present state through a strategy centered wholly upon *production* itself. The managers of today's enterprises have remained aloof to any direct concern with the building of the economic power of the consumers to consume. In fact, management's basic strategy does precisely the opposite.

No criterion of management competence is more devoutly respected than the minimizing of cost through the reduction of unit labor costs—the elimination of employment. Eliminating employment not only maximizes the productive input of the nonhuman factor, for which management feels a special responsibility; it also eliminates toil, a side effect which management quite properly regards as beneficial.

Another equally respected and observed rule of management strategy is to so finance the new capital formation of the enterprise as to avoid acquiring new shareholders, and to minimize the extent to which earnings are paid out to the existing shareholders. As Adolf Berle pointed out long ago, dividend policy of the modern corporation consists of paying stockholders the minimum required to keep them out of court.[66] As the rights of stockholders to demand payment of the wages of their capital have continued to deteriorate, modern enterprise has quite fully closed the door to the accession of new stockholders. We have already noted that less than half of one percent of new capital formation of business corporations in recent years has been financed through the issuance of new equities, and even this is sold to buyers with accumulated financial savings. If the corporate strategy that has dominated private enterprise in the industrialized, non-socialized economies of the world is followed through to its ultimate goal, either most of the populations of these economies will starve, or their income will be redistributed according to need, as much of it is today.

The extraordinary thing about the incomplete strategy of business is the extent to which economies (particularly that of the United States) have succeeded thus far, in the face of this constant short-circuiting of purchasing power, in reaching modest growth rates and creating a narrow but significant pinnacle of affluence. The longer-range cost of this short-range success is difficult to assess and, in fact, may never be known. It must be measured in terms of general affluence *not* created, enjoyment thwarted, leisure unrealized, economic insecurity that need not have been, deterioration of the property system that should not have occurred, public and private debt accumulations that continue to grow at accelerated rates but which should have disap-

peared long ago, labor and civil strife that should not have
occurred, the nonabsorption of technological innovation
into the economy, new capital formation that did not take
place, resources wasted in attempting to redistribute income in traditional one-factor economic patterns, military
engagements triggered by an excess of munitions produced
to create full employment prosperity, demoralization, confusion, and disorganization. As business strategy expands
production and contracts the power of consumers to buy
the goods and services produced, government fills the purchasing-power gap in all the well-known ways.[67]

Corporate strategy implicit in the theory of universal
capitalism can within a reasonable number of years release
these accumulated tensions and correct these economic and
social distortions. Corporate planning that takes into consideration not only the necessity for maximizing production
of goods and services, but also maximizing the participation
of all consumers in production in order to enable them to
enjoy consumption, can unleash productive forces inherent
in technology that are powerful enough to erase the monu-
mental mistakes of the past and present.

Business planning under universal capitalism will shift
the bulk of all economic planning functions to business
leadership and to the leadership of the successor to today's
labor organization. Labor organizations of the future will
be designed to increase the individual's participation in
production not just through his employment, but through
his individual capital ownership as well. Government will
retire to the "umpire" position, making certain that equality of economic opportunity (not just *employment* opportunity) exists, policing market competition, and policing
the concentration of individual productive power.

The minimizing of unit labor costs by business will not
only continue, but will accelerate, and labor as such will

welcome it. But the worker or former worker's participation in production through his ownership of the nonhuman factor of production will grow. It is in this manner that business must build its own markets, and the economic power of individuals both to produce general affluence and to consume the goods and services at generally affluent levels.

Corporate planning increasingly will be occupied with the expansion of production, technological innovation, and the reduction of costs and prices. It will be decreasingly occupied with the internecine warfare for perpetually inadequate consumer purchasing power and redistributive labor strife. It will be absorbed less in production for governmental use, and more in production for private use. Corporate planning will become increasingly effective as future costs are relieved of the distortion resulting from gorging labor costs with welfare.

The extension of domestic enterprises into foreign economies will be undertaken with full awareness that increased productive power in *those* economies must also be accompanied by increasing the economic power of *their* citizens to consume. This can only adequately be accomplished if new capital formation in the host economies is financed in ways that enable an expanding proportion of their populations to participate in production through the ownership of the nonhuman factor as well. If the corporation wishes to produce on foreign soil, it must have constituents there whose power to consume is commensurate with the power of their economies to produce.

PART IV

Summation of the Case

23 THE PRODUCTION ETHIC
OF UNIVERSAL CAPITALISM

EACH NATION, singly or in alliance, is facing an economic crisis rising out of the incompatibility of pre-industrial political-economic concepts with the facts of industrial life. The politico-economic ideas upon which the invisible structures of the world's economies are built, those of the free world as well as those of the communist world, assume and teach that labor is the only factor of production. But the facts of industrial life happen to be that in an advanced industrial economy—which all nations either have or seek —capital produces most of the goods and services. Were it not for the disruptive problems created by the massive misconceptions of one-factor thinking, the nonhuman factor of production would produce even more of the aggregate output.

In the United States and Canada, in the European and Latin American countries, in Japan and in other countries that pretend to have capitalist economies, there is no rational concept of a capitalist economic system *qua* system. For the word "system" implies logic, and there is no logic in looking to full employment as the sole mechanism for enabling the masses to participate in production, where the bulk of the wealth is produced, as it is in the already industrialized countries, by the nonhuman factor of production.

In none of these economies is genuine affluence enjoyed by any except those at the economic pinnacle of the society. In none does any leader have the courage or audacity to announce that the proper goal of the economy is *general affluence;* for affluence is the product of capital, not labor, and the capital owners whose holdings are of sufficient size to yield them affluence are an infinitesimal portion of the populations. In none of these economies, though all are dominated by the Puritan Work Ethic or its moral equivalent, has this dominant ethic been reconciled with the system of industrial production. Only the concept of universal capitalism updates the work ethic into a rational *Production Ethic.* In none of these economies is there the faintest recognition that if it is important—both to motivate the production of general affluence, and to maintain peace, law and order in an economic society—that men produce the wealth they need or desire to enjoy, the proportion of men who engage in production through ownership of the nonhuman factor must grow in concert with the relative productive output of capital. That logic is provided only by the concept of universal capitalism.

Discourse on "tools," "investment," the "investment function" of the owner of concentrated financial savings, the "job-creating magic" of financial capital, or the sacrificial beneficence of the owner of concentrated savings for "risking his savings,"[68] belongs to the pre-industrial age of one-factor thinking. It is no substitute for recognizing that the nonhuman factor produces wealth for its owners in precisely the same physical, economic, political and moral sense as the human factor. Nor is it a substitute for recognizing that if there is indeed a right to life and liberty in an industrial society, then it is the heritage of every man to own a viable share of the factor of production that is the chief source of life and the chief bulwark of liberty in that society.

24 MOUNTING ECONOMIC UNEMPLOYMENT: A CRISIS

As THEY ALWAYS DO on the threshold of every great crisis, those in charge of the power structure—the establishment—are losing no opportunity to proclaim that the economy of the United States has been manipulated by the Keynesian techniques of the "new economics" to a state of self-renewing perfection. The din of this self-congratulation mounts in step with the accumulating evidence of impending economic disaster. Let us examine a sampling of the evidence.

Economic employment is employment in the production (including, of course, distribution) of goods and services that provide men with creature comforts. Any sensible definition of economic employment would also include, in addition to the maintenance of normal government functions, the employment required to supply national defense needs that are reasonable in the light of world conditions, and to construct public works that are democratically approved by vote of those who are to be charged with the expense.

But the term "economic employment" requires also a definition of noneconomic employment. *This is employment created for the sake of the employment itself.* It is nonleisure employment that is not necessary or not used to add to the production of goods or services that minister to creature comforts in demand by individuals in the market place, or for the maintenance of civil government, or for the building of reasonable national defense, or for the building of democratically approved public works. It is make-work employment.

The marvelous success story of the Keynesian new economics is built upon the suppression and obscuring of the distinction between economic employment and noneconomic employment. It measures national economic performance by the degree to which the economy achieves *undifferentiated* full employment and by the annual increase in the market value of the goods and services produced. The increase may represent goods and services that are utterly useless to man; they may even consist of goods and services that are intended to do nothing but to kill, cripple, starve and mutilate innocent men, women and children, and to squander precious natural resources in the process.

Since employment statistics are kept in such a way as to make impossible any precise measurement of economic and noneconomic employment, it is necessary to estimate the extent of make-work employment in the United States at the present time. We believe that the following estimates are conservative. All estimates are rounded and approximate. They are based upon an estimated labor force of eighty million persons.

Table 1. ESTIMATED NONECONOMIC NONLEISURE
EMPLOYMENT IN THE UNITED STATES

Employed in the production of excessive military goods not actually needed for national defense, including employment supported by the space race that cannot be justified under present world economic conditions except as a military measure, and as such it is simply celestial make-work   10,000,000

Employed on farms due to government subsidy of the production of surpluses for which there is no economic market demand   2,500,000

Employed in the performance of "pretended" work that would be called featherbedding if the social pressure to conceal this popular form of needist redistribution did not prohibit use of the term   4,000,000

Employed in federal and state government-subsidized public works that would not be built under prevailing economic conditions except to "create" employment 3,000,000

Employed in federal, state and local government jobs administering the towering framework of needist redistribution, all of which would be neither necessary nor tolerated in a universal capitalist economy which distributed general affluence automatically through the participation of all households and individuals as workers and/or capital owners in the production of useful goods and services[69]   3,000,000

Employed in the production of goods and services purchased in the United States but given away under the various foreign aid programs of the United States 1,000,000

Employed in the military service, beyond the number of troops (approximately one million) that would constitute an adequate military force in a peaceful world in the process of solving its economic distribution problems by the orderly processes of the Second Income Plan. Oddly enough, the same pre-industrial economic concepts that prevent economic growth rates of 15% to 20% per year (by simultaneously raising the power of the masses to consume as productive power is raised) also leave little opportunity but military activity to keep

poverty-stricken and restless people distracted from
economic revolution   2,500,000

Total noneconomic employees (i.e., economically unemployed, but counted in U.S. government statistics as
employed—in any event, not included among the "unemployed")   26,000,000

If we add to this total of the economically unemployed
the four million persons government statistics *admit* to be
unemployed, it becomes clear that the number of workers
actually employed in the economic sense in the United
States is about fifty million, and the number of economically unemployed becomes thirty million, or 37.5% of the
labor force.

Once the distinction between necessary and unnecessary
(or make-work) employment is made, we are in a position
to see some of the more frightening aspects of operating
an industrial economy on pre-industrial economic theories.
Clearly, such an economy is guilty of the most licentious
and extravagant waste of resources in history, at a time
when it is becoming increasingly clear that the resources
of the world, and particularly those of the United States,
are not unlimited.

Clearly, too, an economy built upon full employment,
when the whole of technology, most of science, and most of
the efforts of management and engineering are directed
solely at eliminating employment, is a *war-prone* economy.
No one would be so rash as to assert that brush-fire wars
like Korea and Vietnam would intentionally be started for
the purpose of fulfilling the promises of a political administration to bring about prosperity through "creating
full employment." But the people of the United States are
morally committed to the private-property principle of dis-

tribution. They believe that wealth or income should be distributed to those who produce or earn it. And where the underlying needist principle of distribution supporting noneconomic employment becomes apparent (as it does in leaf-raking, pork-barrel public works, producing surpluses that have to be stored and periodically given or thrown away), it becomes increasingly difficult to get appropriations from Congress and from legislatures to support such make-work.

On the other hand, it is relatively easy, playing on primitive emotions, to get the military appropriations that are actually the best Keynesian expedient for contriving toil. These appropriations tend to maintain full employment and yet result in the production of no useful goods or services that might compete with the civilian economy.

But the size of military appropriations grows apace as technology reduces the labor input per unit of output in every industry and enterprise. Doubts begin to arise that even these appropriations may *exceed* the actual military requirements. Even so high an official as the Secretary of Defense of the United States, in an unguarded moment may remark, "A nation can reach the point at which it does not buy more security for itself simply by buying more military hardware—we are at that point."[70] People close to the picture write books with titles like *On Thermonuclear War*,[71] *Kill and Overkill*,[72] *In the Name of Science*,[73] *Our Depleted Society*,[74] *The Warfare State*,[74a] etc. Clearly, in order to maintain the hoax of a full employment industrial economy, and to keep the legislative appropriations flowing through which this shameful squandering of resources, human vitality and technical know-how can continue, the fear of the legislator must be directed toward a *clear and present danger*.

For example, within moments after President Lyndon

B. Johnson returned from a peace-seeking (and hence potentially full-employment-killing) Manila conference in November, 1966, Secretary of Defense Robert S. McNamara announced, not unpredictably to those familiar with the ritual, that there was "considerable evidence" that the Soviet Union was "building and deploying an anti-ballistic missile system" and that he planned to recommend to Congress that the United States begin production and deployment of the Poseidon missile at a cost of two billion dollars in initial expenditures, and an estimated cost for the program of thirty billion dollars. Three days later a leading San Francisco newspaper came out on cue with its solemn endorsement. "The price of assuring freedom is truly staggering," it editorially intoned, "but the alternative is unthinkable."[75] What is truly staggering, of course, is the price of assuring full employment; logical economic thought being the unthinkable alternative.

An economy that must depend upon military and space expenditures to create employment is war-prone. Caroline Bird wrote in the last chapter of *The Invisible Scar:*

> Opinion divides on how much defense we need, but the Depression-bred see no way out of an agonizing choice between unemployment and the risk of atomic war. The choice is confused because no one wants to put it that bluntly, and only the specialists have learned to accept the enormity of atomic war. To men of policymaking age, the word "war" means the war that ended the Depression, a wonderful bonanza for everyone.[76]

25 THE DEBT FOUNDATIONS
OF THE BOOM MIRAGE

DESPITE THE DANGERS and moral imperfections inherent in a full-employment policy, we wish to rest our case for the adoption of a policy of universal capitalism in the United States and for the elimination of all needist expedients (as rapidly as orderly reform and the preservation of a growing income flow to all families will permit) essentially on economic grounds.

An economy in which only fifty million persons out of a labor force of eighty million are producing useful goods and services and thirty million are economically unemployed (even though most of them are physically occupied in noneconomic jobs that obscure the facts) can never be a generally affluent economy. Only 10% are affluent, and 90% are impoverished to degrees that increase in severity as one scans the economic pyramid from top to bottom. Twenty-six out of the thirty million waste their time, the resources they work with or on, and their skills, in order to legitimate their claim to a paycheck. They must do this because they cannot participate, through ownership of capital, in the production of useful goods and services as they are produced under the current state of technology in the United States. Twenty-six million workers are compelled to produce useless goods and services, because the obsolete economic concepts upon which our invisible structure is built do not enable them to produce useful ones. This is an economy designed to create poverty for the majority, not general affluence.

As public and private debt (owned entirely by the top 10% of wealth holders) mounts upward from the one and a half trillion-dollar level to support this grotesque arrangement, the claims of the few upon the future productive power of the many and the future productive power of the nonhuman factor threaten the legal foundations of the economy. Viewed in the light of the concept of universal capitalism, the debt structure of the United States has a vastly different significance than that popularly attributed to it:[77]

(1) three hundred and sixty-two billion dollars of federal and state debt is a measure of the governmentally accomplished needist redistribution primarily from the capital owners to the nonowners of capital. The ownership of the great bulk of these debt claims lies in the upper 3% of wealth holders; virtually all of it lies within the upper 10%.

(2) four hundred and forty-six billion dollars of corporate debt represents, for the most part, the extent to which new capital formation is financed in ways which assure that it will be owned by the top 10% of wealth holders who today already own all existing capital within the economy.

(3) four hundred and sixty billion dollars of personal debt of individuals for the most part represents an attempt to close the purchasing power gap between the income received by individuals and the market value of the goods and services which producers are straining to sell.[78] As we have already pointed out,[79] consumer credit and housing credit are inherently incapable of closing *any* purchasing

power gap. They only make the gap bigger to the extent of the interest charged on the loans.

Rising aggregate debt, public and private, is thus largely a means of disguising the political, economic and social consequences of building the invisible structure of our economy on one-factor concepts in a two-factor world. It is also a means of accumulating economic strife and dislocation and passing them on to the future. By then, hopefully, present political administrations and present generations of educators and business leaders will, by one means or another, have escaped "accountability." The cost of substituting an expedient for rationality in the political affairs of the nation will fall on others. The responsible leadership, self-conferred laurels intact, will be resting peacefully in the grave.

26 THE ABDICATION OF
UNITED STATES INTERNATIONAL
LEADERSHIP

FROM THE BEGINNING of United States' history down to
the close of the nineteenth century, the frontier offered to
men and women born with no property except their labor
power, the opportunity to acquire capital ownership in the
form of land. That opportunity motivated the building of
the most powerful economy on earth. The momentum of
that two hundred-year period was so great that the U.S.
economy has been able to withstand the counterforces of
needist redistributive measures that have been battering
it since 1932. The cost of these degenerative steps, however, must be measured in terms of wasted effort, billions
of dollars of resources squandered in make-work and unnecessary war material, billions of hours of skills devoted to
humanly useless ends, and an incalculable amount of military strife that is *economically necessary* because of our one-
factor thinking.

The settling of the West provided economic lessons for
the world that have yet to be generalized to fit an industrial
age. When land was the principal form of the nonhuman

factor of production, access by the propertyless to land, mineral resources, and timber resources demonstrated, largely by accident, the importance of a property relationship between individuals and *both* factors of production. As the value and productiveness of fabricated capital instruments began to outdistance land,[80] and as the access of the propertyless to land itself ended with the closing of the frontiers, there was no theory of universal capitalism to guide men in the design of the invisible structures of their economies.

As a consequence, the United States has no rational theoretical conception of how it arrived where it is. Not understanding the principles by which it rose to pre-eminence, it does not know how to maintain its position in the present or to extend its success into the future.

In the field of socio-economic goals, it has fallen into that slough of despond, "full toil for all forever." That the political-economy of the U.S. has no lessons to proclaim to the world, that it provides no model to follow, no rationale even upon which to maintain its own efficient progress, has been lamented by almost every serious student to ponder the problem. Here are a few of their comments:

> In an age of science, change is so vast and so violent, that it is easy to become obsessed with the results and to forget either the goals or the minds back of them . . .
> We require political inventiveness which in some way matches the scientific inventiveness of this age. How can we tolerate a world in which everything changes . . . and only civic life remains unchanged, to founder because it cannot cope with its environment? . . .
> If we can produce a generation determined to design goals for man's best life on this planet, if we can educate a generation capable of achieving these goals, if we can keep our eye on the individual and his mental, social, spiritual growth, we may raise new currents in the flood of circum-

stance and, who knows, we may harness high tides to the great good of people yet to be born.[81]

You are advancing in the night, bearing torches toward which mankind would be glad to turn; but you leave them enveloped in the fog of a merely experimental approach and mere practical conceptualization, with no universal ideas to communicate. For lack of adequate ideology, your lights cannot be seen.[82]

There is widespread recognition that the performance of our economy these past several years has been inadequate and that we need new policies to foster more rapid growth and fuller use of our productive potential. Many of the remedies being offered today are revivals of schemes which experience has tested and found wanting. Expansion of the public sector through bigger Federal spending financed by rising debt; injections of spending power into consumer hands through tax cuts or bigger welfare payments; easy credit and low interest rates in the hope that people will spend more from borrowed money—all these schemes fail to come to grips with the fundamental motivations of human effort. At best, they can produce only an artificial stimulus which wears off like a drug unless applied in bigger and bigger doses.[83]

The attack on the capitalist apologetic of the nineteenth century has been successful, but a satisfactory contemporary apologetic is still to be created.[84]

The first half of the twentieth century presented the West with an interesting paradox. The period has been fertile and bold beyond belief in producing hypotheses in physical science. It has produced no correspondingly great hypotheses in the field of economics or in politics.[85]

. . . The time has come to provide the American experiment with a comprehensive and well considered statement of its objectives and its significance. . . Too long our great experiment has been merely the product of conditions without the stimulus and guidance that can be provided only by a well expressed philosophy. We shall accomplish more effectively what we are trying to do if we can have a greater awareness of our objectives.

Furthermore, a well expressed and well understood philosophy will help us to see more clearly the deficiencies in our accomplishments. It will force us to consider whether we are giving too much attention to acquiring things and too little attention to developing men. It will give us tests by which to appraise institutions and policies. It will help to overcome selfish obstacles to the experiment.[86]

In Madagascar, I was aware of the lack of leadership and creative ideas among the Americans there. They spent the majority of their time in forming a "good image" of America and being "liked" by the local people, but they had no social or economic plan to offer, and, in private, agreed that the island would "go Communistic in five or ten years." It really was discouraging.

Also, as facilities engineer, I hired and fired local people. For every man I hired, I turned ten away. I thought to myself, when I cannot offer a man a livelihood, I am, in effect, saying that our "way of life" excludes him. It takes no great savant to know that eventually these people will reject us and our economic system.[87]

One of the most distressing facts about our economic order is that it is not really spreading into the rest of the world. It is not a dynamic, contagious system. There is indeed a "new American capitalism" but it is beleaguered on its little island in a socialist sea. . . . I am affirming that in relative terms, our free economic system does not possess the missionary zeal, the drive and force, the contagion, which it deserves to have . . . We lack a body of doctrine. . . . We lack revolutionary zeal. And all of this, it seems to me, stems from our failure to define our values accurately.[88]

Gentlemen, let us ask ourselves this question: What has caused so many young nations to embrace political beliefs which are anathema to our way and to your way of life?

Political policies which have so often reduced the countries on which they have been imposed to economic chaos and caused their peoples to lose their personal liberties. The wealthy countries may regard such instances as induced by subversion imposed on ignorant people—that, however, would be a superficial examination.

The wealthy countries might ask how is it that their own success and wealth have not been adequate examples for new nations to follow?

The fact is that wealthy and successful countries do not as a rule provide acceptable examples to poor countries.

To a poor man the sight of a millionaire making another million may incite envy; it does not, however, induce emulation.

To a poor man the sight of a poor man improving his condition, particularly if he does this by his own efforts, is an example; for the man who is still poor can picture himself in the position of the poor man who is succeeding.

So, too, to a poor country. The sight of another country with approximately similar conditions making good and developing itself is something which will be closely watched and likely followed.[89]

In this fearful age you must transcend your system: You must have a message to proclaim to others: You must mean something in terms of ideas and attitudes and a fundamental outlook on life: And this something must vibrate with relevance to all conditions of men.

If the businessman and the communist meet a neutral, that is one who is equally open to both, which will impress him more?[90]

In failing to probe the inner nature, the necessary operating principles of a free industrial society; in responding only with dumb spectatorship to the glaring paradox of an industrial economy capable of producing sufficient real wealth to support general affluence but which continues to distribute, decade after decade, only limited affluence; in experimenting with welfare and redistributive measures that affront all human dignity, disorganize the society, and pit man against man, power bloc against power bloc, and push us ever closer to a totalitarian government in which unmatchable power—political and economic—is combined in the hands of the government bureaucracy, the United States is abdicating the responsible leadership which it has, largely by accident, achieved.

We submit that *universal capitalism is the rationale of a free industrial society,* and that in understanding, applying, and teaching that rationale, the United States can again become a leader that truly leads by inspiring, as it once did, the minds and the hearts of men.[91]

27 THE RISING SONS

WE HOPE that this essay has contributed to an understanding of the cost industrialized countries are incurring through the persistent blindness of their leadership to the rationale of a free industrial society, and of the coin in which payment will be exacted. Since the very purpose of an expedient, as opposed to reasoned action in harmony with relevant and sound principles, is to temporize, to gain time, to push the dislocations and problems downstream to those who come afterward, guardians of the status quo will probably escape the consequences of their leadership. They can say with Louis XV, "*Après moi, le déluge.*" Therefore, it is unlikely, although not impossible, that changes and innovations will be *initiated* by the exponents of the "conventional wisdom."

Our hopes of change will be more realistically placed in those who will have to pay the full cost of economic mismanagement. To identify them takes no special prescience. They are the ones who must always suffer for defective economic institutions—the propertyless of all ages, but most particularly and immediately, their children.

In the United States and in Canada, in Great Britain, in the continental countries, in Scandinavia, in Latin America, in Japan, in the Middle East, in the USSR and in the Soviet satellites, in the Philippines and in Indonesia, young people are manifesting their despair over the future their elders are preparing for them. Although these societies are very different materially and politically, in each the attitudes of the young are strangely similar. The young are rejecting the societies in which they were nurtured. Everywhere they are declaring themselves to be alienated from the values of their elders, and contemptuous of the elders themselves. While Western youths imitate the methods they have seen their elders employ to force income redistribution, their sit-ins, teach-ins, protest marches, mass confrontations, student strikes, school boycotts, and other methods of mass coercion are not intended to serve economic ends. Rather they are intended to communicate moral displeasure. Young people are protesting, in the only way available to the poor and the powerless, the cosmic perversion of human values that has come about through society's indifference to the law of urgent and important, and to the multitude of grotesqueries arising out of the elders' attempts to impose one-factor institutions upon a two-factor world.

Apologists for the elders reply that hostility between youth and age is normal, and that the present conflict is simply the old generational rivalry disguised in contemporary issues and rhetoric.

But that is not quite the truth. In the past, youth's criticism was tinged with envy. Between the lines of its bill of particulars could be read impatience to replace the incumbents. Youth was eager to oust bumbling age in order to assume age's power and prerogatives. It also burned to show age how much better a job youth could do. The young were junior members of the club; their criticism had the quality of loyal opposition.

Today's rebellious young people do not identify with their elders; they show little enthusiasm for either emulating them or supplanting them. On the contrary, they seem to view both prospects with distaste. They equate leadership with venality, if not outright villainy. As those who sense catastrophe have always done, they take refuge in escapism. The other-worldliness of many young people, as well as the super-worldliness of others, the rise of sensory pleasure cults, the reappearance on city streets of the unkempt medieval-type mendicant—these are symptoms of a fundamental loss of confidence in society's institutions and leadership, and hence loss of faith in the future.

To uncomprehending elders, the grievances of the young seem vague, their criticism peevish, and their aims, if any, visionary. Nor are the elders especially amused at having their authority challenged by tactics which mimic their own economic behavior in enforcing coercive redistribution. That the young have difficulty in articulating their hopes and fears is true. Their inexperience, their inability to distinguish the fragments of truth from the stupefying deluge of false and misleading ideas that inundates them along with the rest of the public, their impecuniousness—indeed, their very youth—make them unsure of themselves and confused. But their instincts are sound. They are being defrauded by the establishments within which they live and by the world community made up of those establishments.

Young people sense that the mission of technology is to deliver man from toil, from poverty, from economic servitude. Those living in advanced industrial countries, particularly the United States, sense that technology is preparing a new soil and climate for mankind; that for the first time in history material conditions hospitable to the development of a rich, humanistic culture are almost at hand. They sense that human clay up to now has been shaped on the wheel of economic necessity, and that this may be why the results are so frankly disappointing. They believe that the limits of human potential have yet to be discovered. They are eager to explore the kingdom within, to learn to know themselves and each other; to feel, respond and become more aware, to experience intimacy; to repair the intellectual and emotional impoverishment inflicted by two centuries of misguided industrialism. Like sensitive individuals everywhere, and in every age, who are not obliged to labor under the yoke of subsistence toil, they are attracted to the world of humanism. They sense in the air the possibility of renaissance, and the prospect exhilarates them.

But the elders, strange to behold, seem to have received the message of technology backwards. Instead of preparing to open the gates of leisure, they are grimly determined to fortify the bastions of toil. From their elders, the young hear that their first concern must be to train themselves for employment, that full employment is society's highest goal and most sacred moral duty; that the great corporations are social benefactors not because they produce useful goods and services, but because they create toil; that those who own the corporations are human benefactors because their self-expanding investments create toil. The young even hear their elders assuring each other that the very function of technology itself is to "create employment," and that as technology shifts more and more of the burden of production onto machines, people must toil harder than ever to keep the wolf of poverty away from their own and society's door.

Nor are the young especially reassured by the forms the employment creation takes. They hear the elders proclaim that full employment is a function of a continuously expanding gross national product. They see the contents of that gross national product. They conclude that the elders apparently do not care about the quality of things produced—that for creating employment and keeping the economy running, napalm is as useful as diesel fuel; bombs as useful as bread; defoliants for destroying the crops of impoverished enemies as useful as fertilizers for increasing the food supply of impoverished friends; guerrilla-warfare-training camps as good as ski resorts, and distant early warning systems that are obsolete before they are built as good as garbage processing plants, water purification systems, and so on. The silent logic of growthmanship is not lost upon the young—they perceive both the results and the inevitable end.

When young people properly turn to the schools and universities for enlightenment and moral and intellectual protection against a state of affairs their instincts tell them is barbaric, they find themselves being mass-processed through intellectual factories to fit the specifications of the total work state. When they seek the liberal education that would help them to understand the world, that would encourage them to develop into highly differentiated individuals, capable of leading intelligent, interested, appreciative lives, they find themselves receiving the sterile training of functionaries. Liberal education, the "knowledge of gentlemen," in Cardinal Newman's phrase, while still defended by a majority of educators, is increasingly unable to withstand the totalitarian demands of the world of toil, and its insistence on vocational education designed to "fill society's needs." The attempt of the educational establishment to substitute training for education, and to justify and explain the perversion, can only mystify and disgust young idealists.

When young people look for teachers to serve as models and mentors, they too often find members of the professional educators' power bloc—modern counterparts of the Sophists with the difference being that the function of the original Sophists was to instruct their pupils in the methods of achieving worldly success, whereas the contemporary reincarnations seem more intent upon achieving worldly success for themselves. Not only are the young confused and bored by the trivial and irrelevant writing and pronouncements emitted by academic careerists in the name of "research" and "scholarship," they are disillusioned by their rare personal encounters with the jet-set professor who, in the words of a dean familiar with the phenomenon, is "on so many panels, has so many consultancies, and administers so many contracts that a student can only talk to him on the way to the airport."[92]

To their Sophist-educationists the young are not unique individuals to be educated to the limits of their capabilities, but human resources to be processed for society's so-called requirements. In the most august journals of the economics establishment, students read that economists "more and more, in fact, are coming to look at education as a kind of capital formation, yielding income increments to individuals and society in much the same way as does investment in nonhuman capital."[93] Distinguished professors of education publicly recommend that the old-fashioned goal of developing each individual child to his fullest capacity be discarded and that education be viewed as an "investment whereby society assures its survival and shapes a more desirable future."[94] And from their parents, the young incessantly hear that a college education is important because it will enable them to compete for a job.[95]

Young people may not have read *Leisure—The Basis of Culture,* but they share Josef Pieper's revulsion for the daemonic phenomenon he analyzes therein: the rise of the total work state, where no area of life is exempt from the claims of work, and all men are fettered to the process of work, to "the all-embracing process in which things are used for the sake of the public need."[96] They are resisting the proletarianization their elders are forcing upon them. Youth is interested in deproletarianization, and the building of the classless liberal society that technology is making

not only possible, but necessary. The young do not understand why they should be harnessed to the process of work
—increasingly trivial, empty and useless work—in order to
satisfy the pre-industrial work ethic which is the core of
one-factor Keynesian philosophy.

The young in the United States see the tentacles of the
total work state reaching out for them in the "service corps"
concept being cautiously but persistently broached by
various government officials. They rightly suspect that the
real purpose of the service corps is not to provide a fairer
or more just alternative to military conscription, but to
engage the energies, and most particularly the bodies, of
those of student age who are not eligible for the military
draft, are not needed in it, or who, in the event of an ending
to the Vietnam conflict, would not prior to the next similar
conflict find "employment" in military service.

Behind the "policy for youth" enunciated, appropriately
enough, by the Secretary of Labor,[97] the young behold the
sinister vision of toil state which the desperate elders are
preparing—at first for the young, but eventually for every
labor-dependent and hence potentially incomeless individual in an economy where the bulk of goods and services
are produced by capital instruments. They suspect that
what the Secretary's new youth policy really means is this:
At that critical juncture in full employment policy when
young people have finished their compulsory schooling and
now demand, as their birthright, the economic employment
they have been assured it is the function of technology and
business to provide, "Opportunity Boards," to use the Secretary of Labor's astounding euphemism, will siphon them
off the labor market into youth-internment centers. And
if a term of two years does not absorb all the extra man-
hours, as it certainly will not, there is no reason why the
term should not be extended to five years, twenty years, or
for life.

A principle that permits the state to compel some people to serve in work brigades in the name of their own and society's welfare is broad enough to compel the service of any or all. Harbingered by such precedents as the Peace Corps, the Domestic Peace Corps, the Teacher Corps, the National Intern Corps (government summer "intern service"), military corps of various kinds, the Poverty Corps, and even a National Senior Service Corps proposed for needy retired people by the Special Subcommittee on Aging, the direction of public policy rightly inspires in the young the fear that the civilization of the United States is in danger of reverting back to the totalitarian past from which the founders of this country led their great exodus.

Nor are the apprehensions of young people stilled by the fact that service in all the corps, save the military, is "voluntary." Their sensibilities have not yet been deadened by the Orwellian euphemisms of the total work state. They know that in the lexicon of the total work state, "voluntary" soon comes to mean "compulsory." Indeed, a careful reading of the text of the Secretary of Labor's talk at Catholic University of America reveals that youth will have the "obligation" to use the so-called opportunities to be provided by the community to toil, to be trained for toil, or to participate in a so-called "service program" (i.e., perform at subsistence pay the toil no organized power bloc wants to do), and that while the Opportunity Boards visualized by the Secretary have no "authority whatsoever to dictate or compel the individual's following one course or another . . . *there would, however, be insistence that he, or she, use the opportunities afforded.*"[98]

Nor is there anything to reassure youth in the fact that the President's National Commission on Selective Service was expected at the time of this writing to reject the service corps concept as too much like Adolf Hitler's police state to say that every man owes his country a year or two of service. This by no means insures that the concept will not be reintroduced at a later date. As the number of economically unemployable young people rises and "retraining" is revealed for the temporizing ruse that it is, and the swelling volume of youth's unanswerable reproaches begins to frighten the elders, the young will begin to hear that a little police-state order and discipline is good for them, or at least an unavoidable evil. Of course the elders, being moral upstanding men, will regret the necessity for the evil, but they will manage to rise above their scruples. As usual, their excuse will be that they have no *alternative*.

Alternative is indeed the crux of the matter, and here it is that youth is vulnerable. For as the elders point out, the posture of moral superiority is easy to maintain from the sidelines, particularly when one's livelihood and education are being provided for by others. But would the young do any better under the same circumstances? *Will* they do any better when their turns come? The answer is that youth would not and cannot, given the financial and economic framework within which the elders are operating. While the moral convictions of individuals are important in the long run, it is institutions that determine the immediate course of events—particularly the institutions of finance.

Not an evil conspiracy, but defective financial institutions and the lack of alternative institutions have delivered us to the door of the total work state. This book has attempted to present the alternatives, founded on the missing logic of an industrial economy. The logic has always existed, like the force of gravity. Had it been discovered by the mercantile economists of the eighteenth century, industrial history would have taken an entirely different turn; Karl Marx would have had to exercise his genius on another subject, and the mounting problems of unsolved poverty would not be menacing the future of youth.

In his superb book, *Of Time, Work, and Leisure,*

Sebastian de Grazia sadly observes that the fathers of our country had no sons. "For the makers of the country, the good life was the life of leisure. They believed in it, and they themselves led such a life as long as they could . . . after them a leisure class could flourish no longer."[99]

The society envisioned by the founding fathers was not the Great Society, but the good society. It was a society strongly influenced by the law of urgent and important. The founders were not only schooled in philosophy and political economy; they were keen students of their fellow men. They did not expect men who were economically dependent to exemplify personal integrity and civic virtue, any more than did Aristotle. When Alexander Hamilton wrote in *The Federalist,* "In the main, it will be found that a power over a man's support is a power over his will," he was reaffirming Harrington's dictum that power follows property. The founders expected that men who had no property would use their suffrage to invade the property of others. They would have been the first to predict that any war on poverty which did not increase the productive power of the impoverished would inevitably become a war on property. And they understood that property is the only power capable of protecting the individual's political freedoms and rights. In a letter to James Sullivan on May 26, 1776, John Adams wrote:

> . . . nay, I believe we may advance one step farther, and af-
> firm that the balance of power in a society accompanies
> the balance of property in land. The only possible way,
> then, of preserving the balance of power on the side of
> equal liberty and public virtue, is to make the acquisition
> of land easy to every member of society; to make a division
> of land into small quantities, so that the multitude may
> be possessed of landed estates. If the multitude is possessed
> of the balance of real estate, the multitude will have the
> balance of power, and in that case the multitude will take

care of the liberty, virtue, and interest of the multitude, in all acts of government. I believe these principles have been felt, if not understood, in the Massachusetts Bay, from the beginning . . .[100]

Land, of course, was the principle form of the non-human factor of production at the time of America's founding, and no doubt it seemed to the founding fathers that the open frontier beginning virtually at their feet ensured ownership of productive land to all who bestirred themselves to go forth and take it. They did not consider that they were being illiberal or repressive in limiting suffrage to landowners. They supposed they had executed a grand design for a generally affluent society in which their sons and grandsons might lead creative lives of leisure.

As available land vanished and industrial capital began to replace this land as the dominant form of the nonhuman factor of production, the propertylessness of the great enfranchised masses has made us retreat from the founders' plan for achieving and maintaining the generally affluent leisure society. Through reinterpreting the Constitution and through legislation that has eroded the institution of private property bit by bit, we have succeeded in proletarianizing society instead. The important thing about us now is not that "We are all Keynesians," but that we are all proletarians and consequently, as Josef Pieper fears, "ripe and ready to fall into the hands of some collective Labour State and be at its disposal as functionaries— even though explicitly of the contrary political opinion."[101]

If the United States has not turned out as the founding fathers hoped and their grand design is coming apart, it is not because they reasoned wrongly, or because they failed to foresee the end of free public land and the rise of the factory system with its teeming millions owning nothing but power to work. It is coming apart because those who came after them, descendants but not true sons, were not able to generalize the principles behind the grand design into new institutions that would do for the society of their own day what those devised by the founding fathers had done for an earlier one.

However, a tree does not die the moment its taproot is cut. Although property is the taproot of civil liberty and the leisured independent life, and the taproot is now perhaps three-quarters severed, the political institutions by which we may change our destiny are still intact. While more and more men are being made dependent on federal largess, directly or indirectly, for their livelihood, untold numbers have had enough of dependency, and are eager for an alternative that could offer them economic autonomy. Nor has the total work state progressed far enough yet to do its deadly work to the spirit, and so contract the lives of the American people that they can no longer imagine significant activity outside the everyday world of toil.

There is still time to build the universal capitalist economy. We believe that vigorous employment of the Second Income Plan can do the job in twenty to thirty years. But the task cannot be trusted entirely to the discretion of the "elders"—the real responsibility rests on men and women with the courage and the will to experiment and innovate the missing institutions that would create genuine economic opportunity for all. This is the work that remains to be done, and those whose futures lie ahead should be most strongly motivated to do it.

The tenor of youth's discontent leads us to hope that in the rising generation the American founding fathers may have found their sons at last. If so, they and their counterparts around the world will begin to dismantle the dreary workhouses the elders have erected, and set about building, in their place, generally affluent leisure societies: the only environment in which man may live in freedom and peace.

Appendix

THE FULL PRODUCTION ACT OF 19——

EXPLANATORY NOTE

The Full Production Act of 19——, although useful as a model for economic policy legislation based on two-factor theory, either at the national, state, or provincial level, has been designed for illustrative purposes to replace the Employment Act of 1946. Since the latter act is generally recognized to be the most important economic policy legislation in the United States, the immediate question arises as to why it should be superseded.

The reason is this: the Employment Act of 1946 is bottomed on one-factor economic theory. It assumes that economic goods and services are produced only by labor, and that capital (the nonhuman factor of production) functions mysteriously to make labor more productive. This is what the "conventional economic wisdom" of our day holds to be true, but in fact, it is not true.

If the function of technology is to shift the burden of production from labor onto capital—that is, to substitute production by the nonhuman factor for human toil; and if the great bulk of our wealth is already produced by capital (rather than by labor), as our eyes tell us is the case, then full employment, even if attainable, *is never enough*. No household can reach its maximum economic productiveness, no matter how many members of it are employed, nor can it enjoy equality of opportunity for personal leisure and economic security, unless it also owns a viable capital estate.

The Full Production Act retains the ethical principle of the Puritan Ethic and of the Employment Act of 1946; namely, that every household should produce the wealth it reasonably desires to consume. Morally, this is beyond dispute. The question is one of means. If only labor produced goods and services, then people could only legitimately produce income through their labor. But if there are two factors of production (and, *a fortiori*, if the tendency of technology is to improve the productivity of only one of them: capital), then equality of economic opportunity clearly means something more than opportunity to obtain a job, and being fully productive in the economic sense means something more than employing only one's labor. This is the ethical import of the Full Production Act, which defines economic opportunity as the right to be productive, either through employment (where the prevailing state of technology requires it) or vicariously through private ownership of the non-human factor of production: capital —or through a combination of both.

The Full Production Act would declare a public policy of extending affluence to all households by raising their economic productiveness. Because the productiveness of labor in general has at best remained stationary through the ages, while the productiveness and relative quantity of capital instruments has been and is constantly rising through technological progress, the one-factor theory Employment Act of 1946 of necessity has been implemented largely by artificially contriving employment for its own sake, and distributing welfare under the guise of higher wages and fringe benefits. The Full Production Act would be implemented to a substantial degree by changes in corporate financing practices and facilitating legislation making it possible for more and more households to increase their economic productiveness through purchasing, paying for, and thereafter employing the private ownership of productive capital in their daily lives.

THE FULL PRODUCTION ACT OF 19—

An Act to declare a national policy (1) on facilitating the full employment (as herein defined) of all able-bodied and competent persons, (2) on the full participation in the production of economic goods by all consumer units in the economy, (3) on the protection of private property in individual labor power and in the ownership of capital as the factors of economic production, and for other purposes . . .

Be it enacted by the Senate and House of Representatives of the United States of America in Congress assembled,

Short Title:

SECTION 1.   This Act may be cited as *The Full Production Act of 19——*.

Declaration of Policy:

SECTION 2.   Congress declares it is the continuing policy and responsibility of the Federal Government to recognize, and to encourage the citizens of the United States to recognize that:

    A.   Man is born a creative entity combining the physical attributes of an animal with the spirit and soul of a human being.

    B.   Man's creativeness imposes upon him the duty and obligation to engage in creative work from his maturity and the completion of his formal education until the cessation of his creative capacity through death or disability, subject only to reasonable respite for rest and recreation, and that one who so engages in such creative work is "fully employed" within the contemplation of this Act.

C. The creative work of man is of two kinds, corresponding in general to the two aspects of man, animal and spiritual: one of these is the work of producing economic goods and services to satisfy man's need for creature comforts and economic security, and the other is the work of producing the goods of civilization which administer primarily to the mind and spirit of man, including the arts, the sciences, religion, education, philosophy, statesmanship, and the like.

D. There are two factors or instrumentalities which engage, or may be engaged, in the production of economic goods. These are the human factor (which is commonly called "labor") and the nonhuman factor (which is commonly called "capital"); that capital consists of all those things which are external to man, are privately ownable under the prevailing system of laws, and which are capable of being engaged in production.

E. The nonhuman factor, as the result of technological advance (including automation), plays (and increasingly since the beginnings of the industrial revolution has played) an expanding role in the production of economic goods and services, while the human factor plays (and presumably will always play) the dominant and unlimited role in the production of the goods of civilization. The purpose and end of all productive activity, both economic and of the goods of civilization, is the consumption and enjoyment of such goods by man.

F. It is the policy of the laws of the United States to assure and protect the integrity of private ownership of the factors of production by the individual citizens of this nation and by others; that in the case of the production of economic goods and services, the functional essence of such private ownership lies in the right and privilege of the individual owner of each productive factor so engaged in production to receive, *as a matter of right,* the entire net product of the thing owned; that this principle of private property is equally applicable to the income or wealth produced by the labor power privately owned by the worker (the human factor) and to the income or wealth produced by the non-human factor owned by the capital owner; that the right and privilege of private property in the means of production is meaningless in a free economy and free society unless the *value* of the income or wealth produced by a factor of production is (except in the case of legally authorized and regulated monopolies) freely and impartially determined by the forces of supply and demand in workably free, competitive markets; that this principle of private property in the means of production is embodied in the principle of distribution of economic goods and services (or their purchasing power equivalent), of the private-property, free-market economy of the United States, which is "from each according to what he produces, to each according to what he produces."

G. The nature and function of technology is to provide the means by which man subdues nature and makes her perform for him the work of producing economic goods and services; that through progress in technology, man transfers the burden of economic production from the human factor (labor) to the nonhuman factor (capital); that the promise implicit in technology is the release of man from the obligation to toil for the production of economic goods and services, and thus to free him to devote ever more fully his energies to the advancement of his civilization through the more disciplined and difficult work of producing the goods of civilization, so that the full employment of man's creative energies must consist increasingly, as technological progress moves forward, in his devoting his energies, efforts, and powers to the production of the goods of civilization.

H. The freedom and dignity of each consumer unit (household) within the American economy, whether it be comprised of an individual or of two or more individuals, requires that each such consumer unit produce, and that it constantly have the power and opportunity to *produce*, within the limits of the overall capacity of the economy the purchasing power equivalent of the economic goods and services which it reasonably desires to consume; that the recognition of this right on the part of each household imposes upon the government of the United States and upon the governments of the several states of the Union, to the extent they shall by appropriate legislation concur herein, a social responsiblity to foster the institutions under which citizens may produce the economic goods and services, and may acquire the private ownership of the means of producing the economic goods and services necessary to provide themselves with individual economic wellbeing and security and to render unnecessary any citizen's being or becoming an object of economic distribution based upon need in any form.

I. The production of wealth (i.e., economic goods and services) is a means to an end, and is not an end in itself; that the human factor of production (labor) should never be considered a "resource" to be "fully employed" in the production of economic goods and services if those economic goods and services can be produced by the non-human factor of production; that the end to which the production of wealth is a means is the living of a good, comfortable, secure, creative and law-abiding life for individual citizens.

J. The market value of the economic goods and services produced by a free-market economy within a given period of time is approximately equal to the aggregate purchasing power distributed as a direct result of the productive process to those who participate, either through employment of their privately-owned labor power or their privately-owned capital, or both, in the process of economic production.

K. Any consumer unit of this economy that consistently produces, either through its privately-owned labor power, its privately-owned capital, or both, wealth and income in excess of what it reasonably desires to consume and reasonably needs to provide it with economic security, under conditions wherein any other consumer units in the economy are consistently deprived of the opportunity to produce sufficient economic goods and services or the purchasing power equivalent thereto equal to what they reasonably desire to consume and to provide themselves with economic security, is thereby seeking to excessively concentrate its ownership of personal economic power to produce wealth and thus to indulge its greed; that it is the policy of the United States to discourage and prevent greed where it interferes with the individual economic productive rights of citizens of the United States.

L. Unlike the production and employment of economic goods and services, the production and enjoyment of the goods of civilization is an end in itself, and the need of society for the goods of civilization is unlimited; that the ultimate goal of a free society is to maximize the production and enjoyment of the goods of civilization, not for economic reward, for they are things that are inherently desirable and that ideally would not be produced for economic reward but for their intrinsic value, for the contributions to society and humanity which they comprise, and for the achievement involved in their creation and contribution.

M. Assuming the availability of land and natural resources, each mature individual other than those who suffer physical or mental infirmity is born with the private ownership of the means (his labor power) to contribute, in a pre-industrial, pre-automated economy, to the production of economic goods and services for the satisfaction of his creature needs and desires; that as technological change moves through the advanced stages of automation, the burden of production of economic goods and services falls increasingly upon the nonhuman factor of production, thus reducing and in some cases destroying the economic productiveness of the human factor of production; that under these conditions, the freedom, dignity and general affluence of individuals requires that the Government of the United States and the governments of the several states of the Union, to the extent that each of them, by appropriate legislation, shall concur herein, promote and foster the institutions under which citizens may maintain and increase their economic productiveness through their lawful and orderly acquisition of increasing quantities of the private and individual ownership of the nonhuman factor of production.

SECTION 3. The Congress declares that it is the continuing policy and responsibility of the Federal Government to use all practicable means consistent with its needs and obligations and other essential considerations of national policy, with the assistance and cooperation of industry, banking, finance, agriculture, labor and State and local governments, to coordinate and utilize all its plans, functions and resources for the purpose of creating and maintaining, in a manner calculated to foster and promote free competitive enterprise and broad, effective, individually-owned, private property in capital, and the institutions and agencies necessary thereunto, and the general welfare, conditions under which there will be afforded full opportunity for every household, comprised of one or more individuals, able, willing and seeking to produce the wealth (income) which its member or members reasonably desire to consume, to produce such wealth and income either through useful employment, including self-employment, or through the private ownership of interests in productive capital, or through a combination of the two, and to promote the maximum production of wealth and income for all households in the economy with a minimum of personal toil and drudgery.

SECTION 4. Economic Report of the President.

A. The President shall transmit to the Congress not later than January 20th of each year an economic report (hereinafter called the "Economic Report") setting forth:

1. The rate of production of economic goods and services, the levels of participation in economic production by the households of the economy, the extent to

which such production is being achieved respectively
through the human factor, and through the privately-
owned nonhuman factor, the levels of purchasing
power of the households of the economy and the extent
to which they result from employment, the private
ownership of the nonhuman factor, and from other
sources, and the levels and composition of production
needed to carry out the policies declared in Sections 2
and 3 hereof;

2. Current and foreseeable trends in the rate of
production of economic goods and services, the levels
of participation in economic production by the households of the economy, the levels of employment, the
levels of capital ownership, and the levels of purchasing power of the households of the economy resulting
respectively from participation in production through
employment, through the private ownership of the
nonhuman factor, and from other sources;

3. The degree to which the value of labor and the
value of the nonhuman factor of production are determined by the forces of supply and demand in workably free competitive markets or are administered,
manipulated or controlled by private persons, by private corporation, or by public agencies, or otherwise;

4. The extent to which goods and services are being
produced by government or government-owned agencies or entities or by nonprofit corporations;

5. The levels of concentration of the ownership
of the nonhuman factor of production, and the extent
to which greed in connection therewith may be impair-
ing the right of all households within the economy to
produce the wealth or income which they reasonably
desire to consume;

6. The availability and adequacy of private and/
or governmental institutions or agencies for facilitating by financing and by other lawful means the purchase or acquisition of capital equities by households
with sub-viable capital holdings;

7. The levels of idleness or failure to engage in creative work within the society, and current and foreseeable trends therein;

8. The extent to which the economically available creative talents and energies of the citizens are fully engaged in contributing to the work of civilization, including the arts, the sciences, religion, education, philosophy, statesmanship, etc., the current and foreseeable trends therein and recommendations for changes or improvements therein;

9. The degree of effectiveness of the laws, both Federal and of the several states, providing for the protection and integrity of private property in the ownership of each of the factors of production;

10. The levels of technological improvement, and the adequacy thereof, under the prevailing state of development in the physical sciences and in engineering to maximize the production of goods and services within the economy with a minimum input of human toil and drudgery;

11. The extent to which wealth and income may be distributed within the economy on the basis of need rather than on the basis of contribution to production, and of current and reasonably foreseeable trends therein and recommendations for the minimization thereof;

12. The levels of technological advance within the various industries, and the current and foreseeable trends therein, and recommendations for the acceleration and improvement thereof;

13. A review of the economic programs of the Federal Government and of the several state governments relating to each of the foregoing during the preceding year and of their effect upon the production of goods and services, the production of the goods of civilization, the minimization of toil, the private ownership of the means of production, the existence of workable and free competition within the markets of

the economy, and upon the existence and extent of idleness or the failure to fully employ the creative talents and energies of the people of the United States, and of the means available for the minimization and elimination of such idleness;

14. A program for carrying out the policy declared in Sections 2 and 3, together with such recommendations for legislation as he may deem necessary or desirable.

B. The President may transmit from time to time to the Congress reports supplementary to the Economic Report, each of which shall include such supplementary or revised recommendations as he may deem necessary or desirable to achieve the policy declared in Sections 2 and 3.

C. The Economic Report, and all supplementary reports transmitted under subsection B of this Section shall, when transmitted to Congress, be referred to the Joint Committee created by Section 6.

SECTION 5. *Council of Economic Advisers.*

A. The Council of Economic Advisers (hereinafter called the "Council") created in the Executive Office of the President by the Employment Act of 1946 is hereby designated as the Council of Economic Advisers under and for the purposes of this Act. The Council shall continue to be composed of three members who shall be appointed by the President by and with the advice and consent of the Senate, and each of whom shall be a person who, as a result of his training, experience and attainments, is exceptionally qualified to analyze programs and activities of the Government in the light of the policy declared in Sections 2 and 3 of this Act and to formulate and recommend national economic policy to promote full participation in the production of economic goods by all households in the economy, broader and more effective private capital ownership, production, the expansion of privately-owned competitive enterprise, the full utilization of the creative energies and talents of all citizens and residents of the United States and its territories, and the minimization of human idleness. The President shall designate one of the members of the Council as Chairman and one as Vice Chairman, who shall act as Chairman in the absence of the Chairman. The incumbents of the Council of Economic Advisers established by the Employment Act of 1946 holding office on the effective date of this Act shall hold such offices in the Council of Economic Advisers hereunder, subject to the provisions of this Act.

B. Employment of Specialists, Experts and Other Personnel.

The Council is authorized to employ, and fix the compensation of, such specialists and other experts as may be necessary for the carrying out of its functions under this chapter, without regard to the civil-service laws, and is authorized, subject to the civil-service laws, to employ such other officers and employees as may be necessary for carrying out its functions under this chapter.

C. Duties.

It shall be the duty and function of the Council:

1. To assist and advise the President in the preparation of the Economic Report;

2. To gather timely and authoritative information concerning economic development and economic trends, both current and prospective, to analyze and interpret such information in the light of the policy declared in Sections 2 and 3 of this Act for the purpose of determining whether such developments and trends are interfering, or are likely to interfere, with the achievement of such policy, and to compile and submit to the President studies relating to such developments and trends;

3. To appraise the various programs and activities of the Federal Government in the light of the policy declared in Sections 2 and 3 of this Act for the purpose of determining the extent to which such programs and

activities are contributing, and the extent to which they are not contributing, to the achievement of such policy, and to make recommendations to the President with respect thereto;

4. To develop and recommend to the President national economic policies to foster and promote free competitive enterprise, full and effective private ownership of capital, rapid growth in the number and proportion of households owning viable capital estates as a means of increasing their economic productiveness, avoidance of economic fluctuations or diminution of the effects thereof, and to maintain the maximum economic productiveness of all households within the economy of the United States either through employment, the private ownership of the nonhuman factor of production, or a combination of the two, as the current state of technology may determine, and thus to promote the growth and expansion of the purchasing power of the households of the economy;

5. Continuously to study and from time to time to formulate and to recommend to the President means for determining:

(a) the actual needs of the civilian economy for employment of the human factor of production after the elimination of all pretended or false employment, featherbedding, or employment which has been governmentally or privately synthesized for the sake of effecting a laboristic distribution of wealth rather than to fulfill an actual need for such employment under the prevailing state of technology;

(b) the size (by dollar value) of capital estate (herein called a "viable capital estate), generally capable, if owned by households of various sizes, of enabling such households to participate in the production of economic goods and services sufficiently to provide a reasonable degree of affluence and private economic security within the capability of the economy as a whole, which determinations shall be for the purpose of fixing from time to time the minimum goal of capital ownership for all households of the economy which it is the policy of this Congress to encourage;

(c) the size (by dollar value) of capital estate (herein called a "monopolistic capital estate"), which, if owned by households of various sizes, would tend to enable them continuously to participate in the production of economic goods and services in excess of a level necessary to provide a reasonable degree of affluence and private economic security and thus necessarily to deprive other households of the opportunity to participate in the production of economic goods and services sufficiently to provide a reasonable degree of affluence and security within the capacity of the economy as a whole.

6. Continuously to study and from time to time to formulate and recommend to the President means for implementing the policy of the United States to foster the institutions and conditions under which households of the economy can build their privately-owned economic power to enjoy a reasonable degree of affluence as a result of their participation in production through their private ownership of one or both of the factors engaged in production, and thereby to minimize the extent to which such households need rely upon any form of social security or socially distributed welfare within the economy.

7. To make and furnish such studies, reports thereon, and recommendations with respect to matters of Federal economic policy and legislation as the President may request.

D. Annual Report.

The Council shall make an annual report to the President in December of each year.

E. Consultation with Other Groups and Agencies;

Utilization of Governmental Services and Private Research Agencies.

1. In exercising its powers, functions and duties under this chapter:

(a) the Council may constitute such advisory committees and may consult with such representatives of industry, banking, finance, science, agriculture, labor, consumers, state and local governments, and other groups as it deems advisable;

(b) the Council shall, to the fullest extent possible, utilize the services, facilities and information (including statistical information) of other Government agencies as well as of private research agencies, in order that duplication of effort and expense may be avoided.

F. Appropriations.

To enable the Council to exercise its powers, functions and duties under this chapter, there are authorized to be appropriated such sums as may be necessary.

SECTION 6. Joint Economic Committee.

A. The Joint Economic Committee, created by the Employment Act of 1946, is hereby designated as the Joint Economic Committee under and for the purposes of this Act. It shall be composed of seven Members of the Senate, to be appointed by the President of the Senate, and seven Members of the House of Representatives, to be appointed by the Speaker of the House of Representatives. The party representation on the Joint Committee shall, as nearly as may be feasible, reflect the relative membership of the majority and minority parties in the Senate and House of Representatives.

B. Duties.

It shall be the duty and function of the Joint Economic Committee:

1. To make a continuing study of matters relating to the Economic Report;

2. To study means of coordinating programs in order to further the policy of this Act;

3. As a guide to the several committees of the Congress dealing with legislation relating to the Economic Report, not later than March 1 of each year (beginning with the year —) to file a report with the Senate and the House of Representatives containing its findings and recommendations with respect to each of the main recommendations made by the President in the Economic Report, and from time to time to make other reports and recommendations to the Senate and House of Representatives as it deems advisable.

4. Continuously to study, formulate and recommend to the Congress means for raising the economic productive power of those households of the economy that are not already affluent, in order thereby to raise their economic power to consume, including, but without being limited to, the following:

(a) promotion of the acceleration of technological progress in the means of producing increased quantities and improved quality of goods and services and the minimization of the use of human toil required for such production;

(b) simultaneously increasing the rate of new capital formation within the civilian economy of the United States and the rate of production and consumption therein of consumer goods and services;

(c) developing means of extending private ownership of capital to a rapidly expanding number and proportion of the households of the economy:

i) through improved and/or new methods of financing the acquisition of equity capital ownership through the use of pure credit in such manner as to create future savings by households devoid of present or past savings, as well as out of current and past savings;

ii) through modifications of the estate and gift tax laws and through discouraging or prohibiting the use of gifts, testamentary or otherwise, or of other practices or devices, to unreasonably concentrate the ownership of capital within particular households;

iii) through methods of financing new capital formation in commerce and industry in ways which enable workers having sub-viable capital estates to purchase and pay for additional capital interests and through promoting reasonable and adequate diversification in such holdings;

iv) through coordination of antitrust policy and the policies hereby declared, including means of financing the purchase by households having sub-viable capital estates of assets of corporations subjected to divestiture decrees pursuant to the antitrust laws of the United States;

v) through facilitating the establishment and financing of new enterprises and the ownership of such enterprises by a maximum number of households theretofore owning sub-viable capital estates;

vi) through the development of a system of investment preferences on newly issued securities of high investment quality for those households which have sub-viable capital estates;

vii) through such other tax, credit, and other devices or institutions as will be effective for that purpose within the policies hereby declared, together with appropriate restrictions on the use of such devices for speculative purposes or to create concentrated or monopolistic capital holdings;

viii) through the primary use of the credit system to promote new capital formation under the ownership of households having sub-viable capital estates, and through a diminishing use of credit to support the purchase of consumer goods and services as the increased participation in production by all households of the economy through increased capital ownership is achieved.

(d) ascertaining and recommending to the Congress the elimination of governmental practices which encourage the concentration of the ownership of the nonhuman factor of production.

5. Continuously to study and formulate means for making effective in both the legal and economic sense the laws of private property as they apply to the human factor and the nonhuman factor of production, including, but not limited to the following:

(a) the elimination, over a reasonable transition period, of the corporate income tax and other taxes which are levied in such manner as to intercept the income arising from production by the nonhuman factor before it reaches the hands of the individual owners thereof, together with adjustments in the personal income tax laws so as to prevent them from raising more than the necessary revenues required by government;

(b) the formulation of legislation designed to encourage or require mature corporations (corporations having reasonable access to market sources of financing new capital formation) to pay out to their stockholders 100% of their net earnings, after setting aside only reasonable operating reserves;

(c) the development and encouragement of freely competitive markets within which the value of the factors of production, both human and nonhuman, is determined, provided, however, that the necessity of maintaining a general high level of purchasing power should take precedence over a competitive decline in the value of the human factor of production where it is not substantially offset by an increased participation of the households involved in the production of goods and services through ownership of the nonhuman factor of production.

6. Continuously to study, and from time to time to formulate and to recommend to the Congress means for facilitating the full employment of all able-bodied and competent persons:

(a) to the extent necessary, under the prevailing state of technology, in the production of economic goods and services sufficient to provide a generally affluent economy; and

(b) to the extent that the production of a high and adequate level of production of economic goods and services can be maintained through the full and effective employment of the nonhuman factor of production and the freeing of a maximum number of individuals from the necessity of performing toil in economic production, in the production of the goods of civilization, including the arts, the sciences, religion, education, philosophy, statesmanship, and the like.

7. Continuously to study and from time to time to formulate and to recommend to the Congress means for extending and deepening the understanding on the part of all citizens of the meaning and implications of the policies hereby declared and adopted.

C. Vacancies.

Vacancies in the membership of the Joint Committee shall not affect the power of the remaining members to execute the functions of the Joint Committee, and shall be filled in the same manner as in the case of the original selection. The Joint Committee shall select a Chairman and a Vice Chairman from among its members. The members of the Joint Economic Committee created by the Employment Act of 1946 who are holding office thereon at the effective date of this Act, shall hold such offices on the Joint Economic Committee hereunder, subject to the provisions of this Act.

D. Hearings.

The Joint Committee, or any duly authorized subcommittee thereof, is authorized to hold such hearings as it deems advisable, and, within the limitations of its appropriations, the Joint Committee is empowered to appoint and fix the compensation of such experts, consultants, technicians, and clerical and stenographic assistants to procure such printing and binding, and to make such expenditures, as it deems necessary and advisable. The Joint Committee is authorized to utilize the services, information, and facilities of the departments and establishments of the Government, and also of private research agencies.

E. Appropriations.

There is authorized to be appropriated for each fiscal year, the sum of $5,000,000, or so much thereof as may be necessary, to carry out the provisions of this Act, to be disbursed by the Secretary of the Senate on vouchers signed by the Chairman or Vice Chairman.

SECTION 7.   The Employment Act of 1946 is hereby repealed.

Notes

(1) *New York Times,* May 14, 1967, p. 1.

(1a) "Foiling Shoplifters," *Wall Street Journal,* Dec. 19, 1966, p. 1. For an alarming summary of the pervasiveness of crimes to alleviate poverty (many of them "white collar crimes"), see the final report of the President's Commission on Law Enforcement and Administration of Justice, published in mid-1967.

(2) John Gunther, "The Overspenders," *Ladies' Home Journal,* April, 1966.

(3) United States Department of Labor, Bureau of Labor Statistics, "Multiple Jobholders in May 1965, Special Labor Force Report No. 63."

(4) *The American College Dictionary* (New York: Random House, Inc., 1963), "capitalism," definitions (2) and (3).

(5) "Weekly Staff Letter," May 25, 1964, (David L. Babson & Company, Boston); *Statistical Abstract of the U.S. 1966,* p. 471, Table 657; p. 472, Table 659; p. 473, Table 661.

(6) "Economic Report of the President, 1961," p. 196, Table C-60; same for 1966, p. 287, Table C-66; "Personal Investing," *Fortune,* May, 1964, p. 75; *Statistical Abstract of the United States 1966,* p. 500, Table 705; p. 472, Table 658.

(7) Some economists have viewed the problem without seeing its implications. See, for example, Robert J. Lampman, *The Share of Top Wealth-Holders in National Wealth: 1922–1956,* National Bureau of Economic Research (Princeton: Princeton Univ. Press, 1962), p. 6: "Presumably, since wealth is a good thing to have, it would be good for all families to have some. Also, it would seem that the wider the distribution of wealth, the broader the political base for capitalism. There is doubtless a maximum degree of concentration of wealth which is tolerable in a democracy and compatible with an ideology of equality of economic opportunity."

(8) Louis O. Kelso and Mortimer J. Adler, *The Capitalist Manifesto* (New York: Random House, Inc., 1958).

(9) Louis O. Kelso and Mortimer J. Adler, *The New Capitalists* (New York: Random House, Inc., 1961).

(10) The Keynesians, particularly J. K. Galbraith, are fond of saying that Keynes, who wholly accepted the outmoded and irrational

distributive mechanics of exclusive dependence upon full employment, disproved the validity of Say's Law. This claim is as naïve and groundless as asserting that the National Aeronautics and Space Administration has repealed the law of gravity. Keynes did not question the identity between "the value of the output" and "the income derived in the aggregate by all the elements in the community concerned in a productive activity." However, reasoning from the false premise that the proper goal of an economy is to arrive at "full employment," Keynes interpreted Say's Law as "equivalent to the proposition that there is no obstacle to full employment." This, of course, neither follows nor is really relevant to the practical life of any society that opens its eyes to the absurdity of the dogma that the function of technology is to "create" full employment. See J. M. Keynes, *The General Theory of Employment, Interest and Money*, (New York: Harcourt, Brace & World, Inc., 1935), pp. 20, 26, 61–65. See also Lampman, *op. cit.*, p. 7

(11) Chen Huan-chang, *The Economic Principles of Confucius and His School* (New York: Columbia Univ. Press, 1911), Vol. II, pp. 483–488, cited in *The World of Business*, Bursk, Clark and Hidy, eds., Harvard Business School (New York: Simon and Schuster, 1962), Vol. IV, pp. 1948–1952.

(12) Josef Pieper, *Leisure—the Basis of Culture* (New York: Pantheon Books, 1952), p. 38.

(13) The motivational value of private property does not seem to depend upon some peculiarity of Western temperament. Writing of the challenge that traditional customs often pose to economic advancement in the developing world, a *New York Times* correspondent from Khartoum recently described how one of the Sudan's leading businessmen overcame the negative economic effect of "the extended family of cousins, aunts, uncles, parents and children (that) may saddle a successful person with a whole retinue of relatives or retainers." Conceding that "the traditional system of having the more fortunate members of the family support their poorer relatives often discourages the ambitious and encourages the idle," Sir Abbas met the challenge "creatively." "In 1964, he set up the Anzara General Trading Company, Ltd., with his own capital, and gave shares in the company to selected members of his family and a few long-time employees, a new twist for all but a few Sudanese families. His idea was to put his relatives to work as part-owners of a family-dominated business rather than simply let them come to him for handouts. Today, this company, engaged in imports and commission work, directly benefits about 70 persons. Mr. Abbas believes his scheme is proving itself not only by encouraging initiative and industry, but also by developing a sense of responsibility among otherwise dependent relatives . . ." *New York Times*, July 24, 1966.

(14) Niccolò Machiavelli, *The Prince* (New York: The New American Library, 1952), p. 90.

(14a) Alexis de Tocqueville, *Democracy in America* (New York: Vintage Books, Inc., 1954), Vol. II, p. 267.

(15) George Orwell, *A Collection of Essays* (New York: Doubleday & Co., Inc., 1953), p. 213.

(16) A far more technically accurate general name for this polymorphic school of economics than "Needism" is "economic communism." Economic communism has nothing whatsoever to do with political communism, or the ideology of any of the socialist economies of nations that identify themselves (erroneously so far as their economic principle of distribution is concerned) as communist. The distributive principle of the USSR, for example, is not communist, but socialist. The Constitution of the USSR states: "the principle applied in the USSR is that of socialism: 'From each according to his ability, to each according to his work.' " Economic communism is only the distant Soviet ideal; it cannot come into existence until socialism, administered by the Dictatorship of the Proletariat, has expunged Bourgeois greed from human nature. But experience has convinced us that if we use the term "economic communism," the confusion with political communism will creep in. So we have chosen the equally functional term, "Needism."

In the *Wall Street Journal*, September 2, 1966, in an article entitled "Our Ineptness Aids Rise of Communism," Harley L. Lutz, professor emeritus of public finance at Princeton University, made an identical judgment. "Just as Russia is moving toward the substance though not the form of a private enterprise society, so we are moving toward the substance, though not yet the form, of a Communist society. A Communist from Mars, looking at the present Federal welfare, Great Society program," states Professor Lutz, "would unhesitatingly identify it with his slogan—'From each according to his ability, to each according to his need.' "

(17) John K. Galbraith, *The Affluent Society* (Boston: Houghton Mifflin Co., 1958), chapter 21, "The Divorce of Production from Security."

(18) See program of the Ad Hoc Committee on the Triple Revolution published in *Liberation*, April, 1964 (Glen Gardner, N.J.: Libertarian Press).

(19) Richard C. Cornuelle, *Reclaiming the American Dream* (New York: Random House, Inc., 1965).

(20) Milton Friedman, *Capitalism and Freedom* (Chicago: Univ. of Chicago Press, 1962), chapter 12.

(21) A.H. Raskin, "Payment by the Hour? The Week? The Year? For Life?", *New York Times* magazine section, Sept. 4, 1966.

(22) Galbraith, *op. cit.*, chapter 21.

(23) C. Northcote Parkinson, *The Law and the Profits* (Boston:

Houghton Mifflin Co., 1960); *In-Laws and Outlaws* (Boston: Houghton Mifflin Co., 1962); *Parkinson's Law,* (Boston: Houghton Mifflin Co., 1957).

(24) *Wall Street Journal,* April 18, 1967, p. 1. According to a Commerce Dept. study, federal civilian employment climbed 10.5% in the year through October 1966 to 2.9 million. State government payrolls swelled 9% to 2.2 million workers; local government employment, at 6.4 million, rose 7%.

(25) The Economic Report of the President, together with the Annual Report of the Council of Economic Advisers, Jan., 1966, p. 89.

(26) In a cover-story on John Maynard Keynes and the Keynesian influence on the expansionist economy in *Time* magazine, Dec. 31, 1965, p. 64 *et seq.*, a sometime-laissez-faire economist, Milton Friedman, in summarizing the influence of Keynes upon professional economists, is quoted as saying: "We are all Keynesians now." This brings to our mind an observation of Schopenhauer's quoted at the beginning of this book.

(27) The economic productiveness of a particular individual may, of course, be increased by his acquisition or perfection of productive skills, through education, training, or otherwise. But there are finite limits within which such improvement can operate, and there appears to be no evidence either that these finite limits have changed within historical times, or that modern production techniques impose higher demands on the human being than earlier ones. In fact, the evidence is that the demands are progressively reduced. This, of course, is what one would expect if he were not brainwashed to believe technological change is supposed to "create" employment or toil.

(27a) Social Credit is an example of the ease with which even one with an engineering background can reach erroneous conclusions by reasoning in monetary rather than real terms. Starting on the firm premises that labor or employment is a means, not an end; that our inability to eliminate poverty is due to institutional rather than physical causes; that the ideal goal is maximum production and minimum toil; that manufacturers and farmers are eager to expand production, and that the bloating of wages and salaries with welfare defeats the cause of general affluence by inflating prices, Maj. C. H. Douglas concluded that the whole problem of the purchasing-power gap could be eliminated by the central government's printing money ("tickets" to consumption) and distributing it in monthly installments through the Post Office as a "national dividend." The propriety of this he defended on the theory (borrowed from Thorstein Veblen's *The Engineers and the Price System*) that because the inventions underlying the industrial arts are the "cultural inheritance" of society as a whole, the ownership of the nonhuman factor (capital) or of an equity in it, should not entitle one to the wealth produced by the thing owned. The fallacy of this idea has been explained by Kelso and Adler in *The Capitalist Manifesto*. (See pages 71–77.) Having been misled into believing that the problem of inadequate purchasing power could be eliminated by means of a superficial monetary device, Major Douglas then was compelled, in the interest of logical consistency, to attack the most fundamental concepts of economic justice and economic motivation. He stoutly asserted that as the non-human factor took over more and more of the productive burden, there need be no relation in the economy between outtake and input; that in a sound monetary system, money is not (imagine!) a measure of value but a mere information system for signaling the need for more or less production; that the legitimacy of the means by which he acquires his purchasing power is of no concern to the consumer; and that wealth produced by capital belongs not to the owners of the nonhuman factor, but to the society as a whole—precisely what the Marxists have always maintained.

Fortunately, the followers of Major Douglas's ideas, mostly in the Canadian provinces of Alberta and British Columbia, have been selective. They have accepted his sound analysis of the defects of conventional economics, but rejected both his corrective measures and his unwitting attacks on private property in capital, economic justice, and economic motivation. See C. H. Douglas, *Social Credit* (Hawthorne, Calif.: Omni Publications, 1924), fourth edition, 1966.

(28) See footnote (10): Say's Law.

(29) Lampman, *op. cit.*, p. 7, cites Jacob Mincer, "A Study of Personal Income Distribution," unpublished Ph.D. dissertation, Columbia University, 1957, p. 136: "The size distribution of income is determined by '(a) the rates of pay received by various agents of production and the extent of their utilization, and (b) the distribution among persons of the ownership of these productive agents. Two classes of productive agents must be distinguished: physical property or nonhuman capital, and human capital representing the productive capacity of individuals.'" The phrase "human capital" is widely used by Needists in their efforts to justify the redistribution of the wealth produced by capital to the nonowners of capital.

(30) Lampman, *op. cit.*, pp. 18–24, 108, 195.

(31) See Louis O. Kelso, "Karl Marx: The Almost Capitalist," *American Bar Association Journal*, March, 1957, Vol. 43, No. 3.

(32) Kelso and Adler, *The New Capitalists, op. cit.*, chapter 4.

(33) Harold Moulton, *The Formation of Capital* (Washington, D.C.: The Brookings Institution, 1935), p. 107.

(34) It should be obvious that consumer credit widens rather than narrows the purchasing power gap. On conventional twenty-five-year installment purchase of a residence, the purchaser pays for more than two houses in order to buy one. And a personal residence is not an income-producing asset!

(35) Kelso and Adler, *The Capitalist Manifesto, op. cit.,* chapter 5.

(36) The other two are the private-property principle of distribution, and the principle of limitation or antimonopoly principle. As to the latter, see pp. 120–121 of this book.

(36a) Addressing a meeting of his cabinet in connection with a decree making broad capital ownership national economic policy of France (*New York Times,* July 13, 1967).

(37) R. W. Goldsmith and R. E. Lipsey, *Studies in the National Balance Sheet of the United States,* Vol. I, Table 11, extended to 1964 by J. W. Kendrick, assisted by A. Japha, *The Morgan Guaranty* Survey, August 1966 (Morgan Guaranty Trust Co., N.Y.), p. 8. While about twenty-five billion dollars of the reproducible assets were residential structures, a substantial portion of these are rental structures and thus properly classified as productive capital rather than consumer goods.

(38) Lampman, *op. cit.,* pp. 21–22.

(39) *Ibid.,* pp. 23, 195.

(40) *Ibid.,* p. 108.

(41) Professor Alfred D. Chandler, Jr. has pointed out that a firm's strategy in time determines its "structure." His use of that term is roughly equivalent to our term "invisible structure." *Strategy and Structure: Chapters in the History of the Industrial Enterprise* (Cambridge: Massachusetts Institute of Technology Press, 1962), p. 383.

(42) *Wall Street Journal,* Dec. 6, 1966.

(43) This is the question asked by Everett E. Hagen in *On the Theory of Social Change* (Homewood, Ill.: Dorsey Press, 1962), p. ix. Professor Hagen states: "The study on which this book is based arose out of the attempt to answer a question which puzzled me during two years as economic advisor to the government of the Union of Burma. The officials of Burma avowed their intense desire for economic development, and there was no reason to doubt the sincerity of their statements. *Why then did they not use the resources at their disposal more effectively toward that end?*" (Italics added.) Professor Hagen concluded the answer lies largely in the field of psychology: personality and personality formation and the social conditions affecting it. Our own view is that in North America, as well as elsewhere, the institutional deficiencies that affect the invisible structure of enterprise are primarily responsible, and that these can be changed by business and government leadership through the strategy of the Second Income Plan. There is, we therefore believe, more hope for creating general affluence in most economies than Professor Hagen suggests.

(44) Lampman, *op. cit.;* Jean Crockett and Irwin Friend,

Characteristics of Stock Ownership (Wharton School Stock Ownership Study, Proceedings of the American Statistical Association, Business and Economic Statistics Section, 1963), pp. 146–168.

(45) Cf. Aristotle, *Politics*, Book I, chapter 9: "Indeed, riches is assumed by many to be only a quantity of coin, because the arts of getting wealth and retail trade are concerned with coin. Others maintain that coined money is a mere sham, a thing not natural, but conventional only, because, if the users substitute another commodity for it, it is worthless, and because it is not useful as a means to any of the necessities of life, and, indeed, he who is rich in coin may often be in want of necessary food. But how can that be wealth of which a man may have a great abundance and yet perish with hunger, like Midas in the fable, whose insatiable prayer turned everything that was set before him into gold?"

(46) See footnote (10).

(47) It is frequently pointed out that the United States was well embarked on its (erroneous) policy of trying to solve the problem of inadequate general purchasing power exclusively through full employment at least fifteen years prior to the adoption of the (Full) Employment Act of 1946 which formally incorporates that policy.

(48) The Employment Act of 1946, Public Law 304, 79th Congress; Hearings, Staff Reports and Monologues of the Temporary National Economic Committee, 1938–1941, 76th Congress; Report of the National Commission on Technology, Automation, and Economic Progress, February, 1966, and Appendix, Vols. I–IV; *Reports of the Commission on Money and Credit* (New Jersey: Prentice Hall, 1963); The Rockefeller Panel Reports, *Prospect for America* (New York: Doubleday & Co., 1961; The Report of the President's Commission on National Goals, *Goals for Americans* (New Jersey: Prentice Hall, 1960); *Goals, Priorities, and Dollars*, Leonard A. Lecht (New York: The Free Press, 1966); and the numerous studies of the Joint Economic Committee and reports of the Council of Economic Advisers dealing with the problem of technology with respect to which the affirmative building of broad capital ownership would be relevant, etc.

(49) Kelso and Adler (*The Capitalist Manifesto, op. cit.*, pp. 171, 256–65) estimated that capital produced at least 90% and labor no more than 10% of goods and services in the United States.

(50) In his budget message to Congress in January, 1967, the President of the United States, acting on the recommendations of the Secretary of Labor and of the Secretary of Commerce (who also announced his intention to return to the well-paid life of a top corporate executive), proposed the merger of the Department of Commerce into the Department of Labor. This is dramatic evidence of how completely one-factor, pre-industrial economic thinking is entrenched in the U.S. economy at this time.

(51) *The Art of Success,* by the editors of *Fortune* (New York: J. B. Lippincott Co. Copyright © 1956 by Time, Inc.), p. 199.

(52) "People," *Time* magazine, July 11, 1960.

(53) See chapter 22, p. 130, *post.*

(53a) See *The New Capitalists, op. cit.,* p. 66.

(54) A *Wall Street Journal* survey of U.S. corporations that are, in effect, operating their own internal banking departments with funds from earnings withheld from shareholders, accelerated depreciation, government tax investment credits, amortization, and depletion allowances, began by quoting a joke, "currently going the rounds in Detroit that General Motors Corporation is saving up to buy the Federal Government." While acknowledging the semi-absurdity of the idea, the article points out that General Motors *was* holding cash and marketable securities of 2.3 billion dollars, an amount larger than the assessed property valuation of 18 of the 50 states; that the cash retained by corporations in recent years has not been matched by needs for new plant and equipment; and consequently, corporations have sought other uses for their funds. Some corporations have simply used their cash to finance seasonal working capital needs previously handled by banks. Others have used funds to purchase their own shares. Still others find it convenient to buy up competitors or to go into diversified lines of business by acquiring companies in other areas of activity. Many have invested in foreign assets and enterprises. A number of corporations have simply spent the funds on capital improvements and expansion, doubtless under some pressure from the U.S. Treasury which frowns upon "unreasonable accumulations" of earnings. ["Affluent Companies," *Wall Street Journal,* Sept. 9, 1963, p. 1.] The present insignificance of newly issued equity stock in the financing of corporate growth is well illustrated by the following extract from a talk by Sidney Homer, a partner of Salomon Brothers & Hutzler, a Wall Street firm specializing in *debt* securities, to the Security Analysts of San Francisco on January 19, 1967: "Four or five years ago in mid-1962, when I first talked to you about the stock market, I discussed money flows and the extreme scarcity of stocks. Let me summarize the points I stressed then. In those days only about $.7 billion a year of net new money was being raised through equities of all sorts in the United States, and this meant that the net money flow into equities from all investors could only be about $.7 billion a year. Add up all the huge purchases of equities by institutions and individuals, odd lotters, speculators, and mutual funds, and subtract all the sales by the same groups, and you came out with net purchases of only $.7 billion. By 1965, the net input had declined to zero. Compare this with $52 billion of net new money in 1965 alone raised through bonds and mortgages. Since 1962, when I last gave you this money flow analysis on equities, the annual volume of net new institutional purchases of equities has risen from $4.3 billion to $6.6

billion, and the annual volume of net sales by individuals has risen from $3.6 billion to $6.6 billion. Since over the years there were almost no net new equities being created, institutions with large receipts of new money and ambitious equity programs could only bid for stocks until they bid them away from private investors. This process has been going on since 1950. Long ago it created an acute scarcity of equities."

(55) The subtitle to *The New Capitalists* (see footnote 9) is, "A Plan to Free Economic Growth from the Slavery of Savings."

(56) It is legally possible, though not presently required by U.S. Treasury regulations, to "pass through" the voting rights, so that the employee, even before distribution of his interest to him, may vote stock held for his account.

(57) In fact there appears to be no impediment under U.S. tax practice in such cases to an arrangement that permits the use of corporate contributions, after the stock is paid for, to be used in part to pay employees second incomes in the form of a specified rate of return on their accounts in the trust.

(58) Kelso and Adler, *The New Capitalists, op. cit.*

(58a) See footnote (64).

(59) Joseph Pieper has addressed himself to this point succinctly: "If the essence of 'proletarian' is the fact of being fettered to the process of work, then the central problem of liberating men from this condition lies in making a whole field of significant activity available and open to the working man—of activity which is *not* 'work'; in other words: in making the sphere of real leisure available to him.

"This end cannot be attained by purely political measures and by widening and, in that sense, 'freeing' the life of the individual economically. Although this would entail much that is necessary, the essential would still be wanting. The provision of an external opportunity for leisure is not enough; it can only be fruitful if the man himself is capable of leisure and can, as we say, 'occupy his leisure', or (as the Greeks still more clearly say) *skolen agein*, 'work his leisure' (this usage brings out very clearly the by no means 'leisurely' character of leisure).

" 'That is the principal point: with what kind of activity is man to occupy his leisure'—who would suspect that that was a sentence taken from a book more than two thousand years old, none other than the *Politics* of Aristotle:" Josef Pieper, *Leisure the Basis of Culture, op. cit.,* p. 43.

(60) Sebastian de Grazia, *Of Time, Work, and Leisure* (New York: The Twentieth Century Fund, 1962), chapter 3.

(61) Robert S. McNamara, Address before the American Society of Newspaper Editors, Montreal, Canada, May 18, 1966.

(62) John Gardner, *Self-Renewal* (New York: Harper & Row, Pubs., 1963.)

(63) *New York Times,* Nov. 6, 1966, p. E-7.

(64) In an article describing the means by which the rich industrial nations, with their heritage of technological know-how, can profitably provide powerful assistance in bringing about the industrialization of the developing economies, but in ways that bring general affluence to the developing economies themselves, rather than preponderant foreign ownership of their productive capital, the authors discussed the tutelary potency of universal capitalism in the world community. See "Uprooting World Poverty: A Job for Business," *Business Horizons* (Journal of the Graduate School of Business, Indiana University, Fall Issue 1964).

(65) Chapter 11, *v.s.*

(66) Adolf A. Berle and Gardiner C. Means, *The Modern Corporation and Private Property* (New York: The Macmillan Co., 1932).

(67) See Part III, *v.s.* The time should come when everyone can see the glaring omission in corporate strategy evidenced by the slogan "An Equal Opportunity Employer," and the symmetry evidenced by the slogan "An Equal Opportunity Corporation."

(68) All of these ideas are facets of that bugaboo, the pre-industrial Puritan Work Ethic. The heart of this nightmare legacy of ours from the past is laid bare by Josef Pieper: "The inmost significance of the exaggerated value which is set upon hard work appears to be this: man seems to mistrust everything that is effortless; he can only enjoy, with a good conscience, what he has acquired with toil and trouble; he refuses to have anything as a gift." *Leisure the Basis of Culture,* op. cit., p. 18.

(69) There are 11.5 million civilian federal and state government employees, of which 2.9 million are on federal payrolls. If one adds the 3.5 million in the armed forces, the total federal and state government payrolls are well over 14 million. This is more than one-sixth of the U.S. labor force. See footnote (24).

(70) See footnote (61).

(71) Herman Kahn, *On Thermonuclear War* (New Jersey: Princeton University Press, 1960).

(72) Ralph E. Lapp, *Kill and Overkill* (New York: Basic Books, Inc., 1962).

(73) H. L. Nieburg, *In the Name of Science* (Chicago: Quadrangle Books, 1966).

(74) Seymour Melman, *Our Depleted Society* (New York: Holt, Rinehart & Winston, Inc., 1965).

(74a) Fred J. Cook, *The Warfare State* (New York: Collier Books, The Macmillan Co., 1964).

(75) San Francisco *Examiner,* Nov. 14, 1966, p. 38.

(76) Caroline Bird, *The Invisible Scar* (New York: David McKay Co., Inc., 1966).

(77) Figures are as of June 30, 1965. *Statistical Abstract of the United States* (U.S. Department of Commerce, 1966), p. 404.

(78) In a burst of rhetorical invention, one organization points to the rapidly accelerating size of this mountain of debt as evidence of the progress of the U.S. economy towards mass ownership of *capital*. But the debt is only capital in the hands of the top five percent or so—creditors—that own it, rather than in the hands of the more than half of U.S. families that are saddled with it! (*Modern-Day Capitalism,* National Industrial Conference Board, N.Y., 1966, p. 19.)

(79) See p. 61, *v.s.*, and footnote (34).

(80) See Chap. 9. pp. 45–46, *v.s.*, and footnote (37).

(81) Excerpts from the address "To Raise New Currents," delivered by President Harold C. Case of Boston University at the Summer Commencement Exercises, Aug. 18, 1962, as reported in *Looking Ahead,* a publication of the National Planning Association, Oct., 1962.

(82) Jacques Maritain, *Reflections on America* (New York: Charles Scribner's Sons, 1958), p. 118.

(83) *Monthly Economic Letter,* First National City Bank of New York, Sept., 1962.

(84) Dean Edward Mason, Harvard Graduate School of Public Administration, speaking about the extent to which the fragmentary ideas of capitalism have fallen before essentially socialistic ideals.

(85) Adolf A. Berle, Jr., *The Twentieth Century Capitalist Revolution* (New York: Harcourt, Brace & World, Inc., 1954), p. 13.

(86) Sumner H. Slichter, in a pamphlet entitled *Technology and the Great American Experiment,* Univ. of Wisconsin Press, 1957.

(87) Ben Hansen, of Towson, Maryland, in a letter to the authors dated May 28, 1966, speaking of his personal experience as an employee of a N.A.S.A. contractor in Tananarive, Republic of Malagasy, Madagascar, Africa.

(88) E. D. Canham, *Harvard Business School Bulletin,* Oct., 1956, p. 6.

(89) Text of a talk by Robert C. Lightbourne, Minister of Trade and Industry, Jamaica, Oct. 26, 1965, at a luncheon in his honor in New York City.

(90) Charles H. Malik, *Fortune,* Nov., 1958, p. 120 et seq.

(91) See footnote (64).

(92) Dean Wesley J. Hennesey, School of Engineering and Applied Sciences, Columbia University, New York, quoted in the *New York Times,* March 7, 1965.

(93) *The Morgan Guaranty Survey,* Nov., 1966, Morgan Guaranty Trust Company of New York.

(94) Paul R. Hanna, Stanford University Professor of Education,

as quoted by Alan Cline, education writer for the *San Francisco Examiner*, December 11, 1966.

(95) Harris Survey, *San Francisco News Call Bulletin*, March 15, 1965: When asked why a college education was important to their children, 74% answered "to get a job." Two percent considered college unimportant. Only three percent of parents answered that college was important "to develop full potential." "Broadening, improves thinking" was the answer of an additional three percent.

(96) Pieper, *op. cit.* See footnote (12).

(97) W. Willard Wirtz, Secretary of Labor, in a talk at the Catholic University of America, Washington, D.C., November 16, 1966. See November 17, 1966, News Release, U.S. Department of Labor.

(98) *Ibid.* (Italics of last sentence added.)

(99) De Grazia, *op. cit.*, p. 414. See footnote (60).

(100) John Adams in a letter to James Sullivan on May 26, 1776.

(101) Josef Pieper, *op. cit.* See footnote (12).

Index

ABOUT THE AUTHORS

Louis O. Kelso received the degrees B.S. in finance, cum laude, and LL.B from the University of Colorado, where he was editor-in-chief of the *Rocky Mountain Law Review*.

Mr. Kelso is the senior partner of a financial and corporate law firm in San Francisco. His own field of specialization is corporate finance. His firm has pioneered the use of highly efficient employee Second Income Plan trusts to enable corporations to finance their growth on pretax dollars and to speedily build equity ownership in executives and other employees.

Mr. Kelso has pursued the study of economics most of his life. His books, *The Capitalist Manifesto* and *The New Capitalists,* written with the philosopher Mortimer J. Adler, were published by Random House in 1958 and 1961, respectively. His articles on the financial, political and philosophical implications of the theory of capitalism have appeared in many learned journals.

Patricia Hetter is a political-science writer. A graduate of the University of Texas, she studied the modern welfare state firsthand for seven years in Sweden. She was one of the few foreigners to make a successful career for herself in the Swedish-speaking business world.

Since 1963, Mrs. Hetter has collaborated with Louis Kelso and is his co-author on a number of articles. She is a director of the Institute for the Study of Economic Systems, San Francisco.